The High School W...

1.) Compare to Career Center

2.) Analogy to sports program! feeder and development.

3.) Bring Media Center into play!

4.) Reduce Plagiarism — (all comp res paper on file)

5.) Cover use student teacher for MCCC and others!

6.) Def on page 56!

7) Ref P. 71 May influence good students to become teachers.

8) p 73 - 5 questions to answer (org plan for proposal)

9) p. 77 3 objectives

10.) p 78 — possible center for publications or college entrance essays etc.

11.) Discuss theory of individualized instruction (see #2)

The High School Writing Center

Establishing and Maintaining One

Edited by

Pamela B. Farrell
Red Bank Regional High School
Little Silver, New Jersey

National Council of Teachers of English
1111 Kenyon Road, Urbana, Illinois 61801

Staff Editor: Robert A. Heister

Cover Design: Michael J. Getz

Interior Book Design: Tom Kovacs for TGK Design

NCTE Stock Number 21187–3020

Library of Congress Cataloging in Publication Data

The High school writing center : establishing and maintaining one / Pamela B. Farrell, editor.
     p.   cm.
    Bibliography: p.
    ISBN 0–8141–2118–7
    1. English language—Composition and exercises—Study and teaching (Secondary) 2. Writing Centers. I. Farrell, Pamela B., 1943–   .
PE1404.H53 1989
808'.042'0712–dc19   89–3003
                                                                             CIP

Contents

Acknowledgments

When I started to dream of creating a writing center for the students I saw five days per week each year, I knew that the most advanced, the least skilled, and the highly creative writers all needed a place for their writing, a community of writers, an ear to listen, and a voice to respond. So did I. My place changed from a shared house on Martha's Vineyard, when I was taking summer writing courses through Northeastern University, to hotel rooms at NCTE conferences, when I was not in my special room at home. My writing community has grown since I began that dream, but I still have the original members at the nucleus of the circle. Tim Donovan of Northeastern University, Susan Kirby of Radford University, and Debby Andrews of the University of Delaware were my ears and voices back in 1981–82 because they have always been dreamers, too. With their encouragement plus the support of my principal, Dr. Robert Nogueira, and superintendent, Dr. Donald Warner, I took the risk, wrote the proposal, and created a writing center. It was, however, the students who made everything work. Year after year, the tutors volunteered their free time because they believed in the project, and the student writers brought even more students to the writing center to become part of this community.

Since then, other members of my writing community have become strong influences on my involvement in the national survey and in the writing of this manuscript. Gary Goshgarian and Peter Stillman have constantly lit firecrackers under me when I lacked the determination or energy to reach higher goals; Bob Parker, L. Jane Christensen, Nancy Sommers, Earl Brown, Sue Hoffman, Lillian Kopenhaver, Bill Speiser, Lil Brannon, Hank Luce, Cindy Selfe, Art Young, and all my special colleagues from the Northeastern University writing program have been the support system every writer and teacher needs. Each contributor to this book proved that writing centers *do* work. Though all have full-time positions, they took the time to write and rewrite their chapters because they believed in this project. Their energy, dedication, professionalism, and willingness to share brightened many a hazy day.

Frequently, we overlook the influence of professional groups that have inspired us much more than we realize. Through the New Jersey

Council of Teachers of English, the National Writing Center Association, the Assembly on Computers in English—all affiliates of NCTE—I have been able to share and learn from colleagues around the world. Through the Woodrow Wilson National Fellowship Foundation and the Geraldine R. Dodge Foundation, I have worked with other English instructors on professional endeavors and been inspired by poets who have shared their sensitivity and vision.

But where would all of this outside support have gone if my colleagues at Red Bank Regional High School had not been supportive of the project? I want to give special thanks to those who put in the extra time and effort to make the writing center a reality, who listened to my tales of woe and suggested alternatives, who took the risks to try new ideas to help their students as writers and thinkers. Finally, the people who have made the most sacrifices for this project, my husband Joe and my parents, deserve the credit for doing much more than stuffing envelopes, licking stamps, and eating fast food. At the end of many a long day, a loving word and a purring Oliver Wendell rejuvenated a most bedraggled soul.

I want to offer a special thanks to John Lansingh Bennett for tactfully guiding me with an effective use of the Socratic method, and to Robert Heister of NCTE for rescheduling my life and bringing laughter into serious pursuits.

1 High School Writing Centers: An Introduction

Pamela B. Farrell
Red Bank Regional High School
Little Silver, New Jersey

Throughout the country, high school writing labs/centers are functioning independently. Some are failing, many are successful, but most are unaware of what other high school writing labs/centers are doing and how they are doing it. Their basic sources of information are books and pamphlets that describe different college and university writing labs/centers, written by college and university professors and/or writing lab/center directors. Although their purposes and philosophies may be similar, the problems in a high school environment are entirely different. For example, tight schedules of classes and the availability of students are only two such problems. Another problem is staffing a center without funds or only with limited funding. Contractual problems present another unique dilemma. As Ellen Brinkley states, "Unlike their college counterparts, secondary teachers usually don't have office hours or classes staggered on alternating days. Instead, they are locked into a schedule that allows precious little, if any, time for individual conferences with students about writing. . . . A writing center can provide that time" ("Roundtable," 1987: 68–69).

I had proposed a writing center at my school in 1981 and found that there was very little information on high school writing centers. Therefore, several articles, including "One-to-One to Write" (Reigstad, Matsuhashi, and Luban 1978) and "Why Don't They Like English?" (Holden 1981), became important in the planning of my school's writing center. The need for models, a supportive network, and collaboration became even more evident over the years. Schools from New York, Pennsylvania, New Jersey, and Virginia sent teachers who were planning to open writing labs/centers to visit our little facility, which I was modifying constantly as space, equipment, and staff improved. Still, every year at the NCTE Annual Convention, I have been overwhelmed by the number of people who need those models, support, and collaboration. In 1986 I decided to attempt to locate and survey as many high school writing center directors as possible, so I contacted Joyce Kinkead, Utah State University, for a copy of the Writing Center Association mailing list and Muriel Harris, Purdue University, for the subscription list of *Writing Lab Newsletter.* As membership cochair of the New Jersey Council of Teachers of English, I also had access to our mailing list. Unfortunately, many people on these lists use their home addresses, so I have inadvertently received several responses from college writing center directors and overlooked names of potential high school writing center directors. On the other hand, some of the respondents have given me names of other writing lab/center directors to include in the survey.

I have distributed over 270 surveys and received responses from more than 100 people, with 70 percent indicating that they either have a high school writing lab/center or wish to start one. Through correspondence with several of the respondents, I decided to write this book, having real high school writing center directors share their experiences. The book deals with problems and frustrations, shares successes and failures, and offers suggestions. In general, it addresses the issue of establishing and maintaining a successful high school writing lab/center. It also provides college and university writing lab/center directors with insight into what the high schools are doing. Perhaps high school tutors who have already been trained may become college writing center tutors, too.

Since the time of my original concept for the book and the subsequent approval of the prospectus by NCTE, I have revised my thinking and rearranged some chapters. I wanted to begin the book with the section entitled "Getting Started," but I did not wish to start or end with theory—we have all read those books! Therefore, I asked a good friend, Bill Speiser, if he would be willing to carry on a dialogue with me in the first chapter of that section. Since we have been commiserating for more than five years about writing across the curriculum and writing labs/centers, I felt that our experiences in trying to establish and maintain facilities at our neighboring high schools in New Jersey would be pertinent. Anyone who has started a writing lab/center can relate to the personal experiences shared in this dialogue; anyone planning to start a writing lab/center should listen carefully to our voices. Many grueling days had been spent editing over forty pages transcribed from the original taped dialogue so that the writers, too, could feel the sense of focus and inspiration for the successful futures of their own writing labs/centers. So, the book begins with a mixture of joys and sorrows, and then moves on to Amy Levin's informative chapter that describes the importance of considering your individual school's philosophy and goals when deciding the purpose and objectives of your own writing lab/center. Amy had researched and visited several writing centers before she established her facility in New York. The next chapter is a truly collaborative effort that attempts to describe the location and design of the space within the writing lab/center. Dick Allen, of Red Bank Regional High School, provided assistance with the writing center layout drawings that were produced by computer aided drafting (CAD). The drawings had been sent to me by several directors. If I were planning a facility now, these diagrams would be extremely important; as one who has a facility, I find them supportive since so many of the designs are similar, though they were created independently of each other.

At this point the reader needs a chapter on staffing the writing center, whether the staff is composed of professionals or peer tutors. Harriet Marcus, who wrote one of the first *English Journal* articles on high school writing centers, shares her experiences at a private school, Oak Knoll, in Summit, New Jersey, while I include information from my survey to describe how centers staffed by faculty actually function. Although Oak Knoll is a small, private school, their credit-bearing course for peer tutors is similar to one offered at larger public schools such as Indian Hill (see chapter 8). Other schools, like Red Bank Regional, can only offer status, college recommendations, and volunteer time for scholarships or congressional awards to peer tutors. After the discussion of staffing, Carol Lefelt and Barbara Brooks explain how to schedule peer tutors or professional staff within the rigid structure of the high school schedule. Scheduling becomes a complex problem in any high school. These two writing lab/center directors share personal experiences to prepare new directors for the adaptation of a schedule that functions in their own schools. Their practical advice and experience are invaluable to directors. Finally, Lil Brannon shares her expertise as a consultant by describing the role of a consultant in establishing a writing lab/center. School districts that provide funds for consultants will discover the advantages of having an objective expert to help create and maintain an effective schoolwide facility.

The second section of the book, "Functioning," gives the reader an opportunity to learn from the experiences of directors who have been particularly successful in keeping their writing labs/centers functioning quite well. "If I had only known then what I know now" is the cry of many who have failed and many of us who continue to struggle each year. This section gives the reader a chance to know *now!* Readers will profit from the discussions by Anne Wright and Elizabeth Ackley, who know how to train their respective staffs. These two very busy ladies are totally involved in their work, yet they found the time to write excellent chapters that tell the reader specifically how they go about training a staff. These narratives offer personal experiences with the training of staff that will prove valuable, whether your staff consists of professionals or peer tutors. Even if directors are called "clinicians" or "coaches" instead of "directors," and even if students answer to "tutee," "client," or "writer," the basic roles are the same. Directors must feel comfortable with the terminology and the training program that works for them.

Section two continues with a discussion of our student clients. Since a staff is useless in an empty room, I asked Jim Upton to share his public relations efforts for getting students to attend a writing center. An enthusiastic soul, Jim offers a variety of suggestions to fill the room. Since all writing labs/centers differ according to school philosophy and goals, Ellen Brinkley, one of the originators of the Madeira High School facility, which was selected an NCTE Center of Excellence, shares her experiences with a variety of students. Then, Sharon Sorenson, a director who created a unique lab with cassette stations, explains ways in which she assists students. Her method proves successful in her laboratory situation. Other writing labs/centers have found techniques to encourage students to become more independent writers and thinkers using trained staff or peer tutors. Many high school writing labs/centers have discovered that staff's and student's working together in a one-to-one or collaborative situation proves successful. Other centers use CAI in ways similar to those used by Sorenson with her audio cassettes (see chapter 18).

From my survey, I discovered two things that must be well managed in order for a writing lab/center to survive: good supervision and organized record keeping. The next two chapters describe both of these. Elizabeth Ackley's honest narrative and Anne Wright's accurate explanation clear up many misconceptions about both concerns.

The third section, "Computers and Other Equipment," details the equipment and computer use of any facility. Administrators want to know what equipment you *need* and what you *want*. The very organized Anne Wright helps us get through that situation. The ever popular concern with computers also enters the picture. Although the emphasis in Anne Wright's essay seems to be on computers, it really describes interaction; the comments are practical from a real situation. The majority of respondents to my survey have computers in their writing labs/centers. Thus, I called upon my own knowledge of the role of the computer in the writing center, plus Pat Stoddart's expertise using computers as writers' aids and Betty Barbara Sipe's personal experience with computer assisted instruction. Whether directors have already purchased computers or are just beginning to select them, they need to hear how computers can be used to fit the philosophy of a particular writing lab/center. These four essays respond to that concern.

The fourth section of the book, "Wider Horizons," presents a collection of narratives that describe ways in which the high school writing lab/center can cooperate and collaborate across the curriculum—with nearby colleges and throughout the community. Henry Luce, director of a college writing center, describes the advantages to both institutions if they do collaborate. Using specific examples from her own writing lab/center, Barbara Brooks shares specific activities that work to offer writing assistance to students in all subject areas. Next, Rosa Bhakuni describes the community connections to her writing lab/center, and John Neil Graham explains the sensitive relationship between his middle school students and the community members of a nursing home. Bhakuni and Graham share some very special experiences. From reading these two discussions, directors may discover connections that would work in their own communities.

Finally, I could not resist calling one of the appendixes, "True Confessions of High School Writing Center Directors." Throughout the development of this manuscript, I received phone calls from contributors who shared horror stories as well as fantasies. High school writing center directors are a unique breed akin to their college and university colleagues. In order to find out specifically what each has experienced, I sent them copies of the interview questions. The selected responses reflect their collective and individual personalities, and so I felt it important to end with their voices rather than just my own.

As I stated at the beginning, there seems to be a need for some sort of network or support system for those who have high school writing labs/centers, both successful and unsuccessful, and for those who wish to establish them. Therefore, I have included a directory of high school writing labs/centers at the end of this book so that readers may contact nearby schools for more information and assistance. This list includes only those schools that responded to my survey, although there are now many more functioning centers. It is mainly a contact list. I hope that this book will be as helpful to all its readers as it has been and continues to be for me.

References

Holden, Robert. "Why Don't They Like English?" *English Journal* 70, no. 3 (March 1981): 16–19.

Reigstad, Tom, Ann Matsuhashi, and Nina Luban. "One-to-One to Write: Establishing an Individual Conference Writing Place at Your Secondary School." *English Journal* 67, no. 8 (November 1978): 30–35.

"Roundtable." *English Journal* 76, no. 7 (November 1987): 68–70.

I Getting Started

2 The High School Writing Lab/Center: A Dialogue

William A. Speiser
Rumson-Fair Haven Regional High School
Rumson, New Jersey

Pamela B. Farrell
Red Bank Regional High School
Little Silver, New Jersey

Farrell: In 1981 you and I met after completing a writing-across-the-curriculum course at Rutgers University. You had a functioning writing center, and I was proposing one. Could you explain how your writing center worked?

Speiser: Sure, but let me give you some background. In 1970, our school had a flexible schedule that allowed instructors to be assigned to resource centers; there were resource centers in English and all other major disciplines. The English center functioned in many ways, one of which happened to be writing conferences. It worked rather well because students had independent study time, and they could either be asked by an instructor to come to the resource center, or they could drop in. Then I participated in the Bay Area Writing Project with Dr. Robert Parker, and got more insight into the functions of writing. Parker and I had a lot in common, and he came to my school to do some research on writing across the curriculum—we wanted to find out how much and what kinds of writing went on in classrooms. We conducted research for two years and provided a series of in-house seminars on writing and thinking for interested faculty. It became obvious to us that, given the school's flexible schedule, it made sense to have a place where writing could be focused on much more intensely. Armed with the research we had gathered, I proposed that a writing center be created.

Farrell: That's when I came to Rumson and you had a notebook with each teacher's name in it. The teachers put each writing assignment in the notebook so that whoever was working with the student could see what particular assignment had been given.

Speiser: That's right.

Farrell: Describe the writing center.

Speiser: It was informally arranged. All writing assignments were jotted down so that, when students came in for help, the instructor who was available could look at that assignment and key into what was being asked. Record keeping was minimal. We were much more interested in the process and had very little to show for the good work we did with students. It was a first-year approach.

Farrell: That was about the same time that I was writing my proposal for a writing center. And we didn't even know we were working on the same goal until you saw my proposal at a writing-across-the-curriculum seminar.

Speiser: Exactly. It was an excellent proposal because you had lots of good information about how to conference with students and how to keep the necessary records most administrators want.

Farrell: Thanks. When I opened the writing center, there had been labs in the school.

Speiser: Labs? What's the difference between a "lab" and a "center"?

Farrell: The labs at Red Bank Regional High School were places where an entire class went. The English department chair plus a clerical aid were there, and the room was used for making up tests or showing audiovisual materials that could not be used in our open classrooms. An entire class moved into the lab facility. It was not geared to tutoring in any way, shape, or form. A few teachers were assigned to the lab, but they did such things as get audiovisual equipment for teachers and administer tests. I began a writing center so that students across the curriculum would have a place where writing was the focus. But unlike you, I could not use the lab facility or the assigned staff. Instead, teachers across the curriculum volunteered part of their lunch period to tutor students under the steps in the media center.

Speiser: I'll bet that that was a good start because the people who were getting involved were interested.

Farrell: Yes, they were, and that year proved there was a need for an assigned space, and that's when my administration gave me the closet upstairs in the media center.

Speiser: I remember that very well.

Farrell: All we had was a desk, file cabinet, little round table, and chairs. We did get an Osborne I portable computer without a printer. At least it came with WordStar word-processing software.

Speiser: Look how far you've gone from there. I remember visiting and looking, basically, at a closet with an Osborne! How did you get students to come to your writing center?

Farrell: I asked students who had been in my classes. Fortunately, I had had a very strong junior honors English class the year before, and I encouraged those students to come for help with their writing. They became good resources because they volunteered the next year to come up and work with students in the writing center during their lunch or study periods.

Speiser: So they were released from study halls?

Farrell: Right. They picked the days to volunteer and soon realized that they could help others, while at the same time use the writing center themselves. Some of them, like Kris Lopez and Jay Czarnecki, learned to use the computer and word processing software faster than I did. In fact, these two tutors even used their volunteer time to earn congressional awards. A nucleus of students, juniors and seniors, then brought in other students who became tutors and stayed with the writing center. I think, through the use of peer tutoring exercises in my own classes, most of these students realized they learned something about their own writing by working with the writing of someone else.

Speiser: So they internalized some of this, and they were able to say, "Gee, this makes good sense."

Farrell: Yes. Many of them were science-oriented students who planned to major in engineering in college, and they felt that they really needed help with their own writing. The best way to do that was to work with students, so they learned the importance of collaboration. I thought that was really interesting. I would like to have had faculty members involved at that point, but there was no released time for faculty members.

Speiser: How were your ideas received by the administration when you first started working on this?

Farrell: Dr. Nogueira, our principal, encouraged them because he knew that some of us on the faculty were interested in writing across the curriculum, and he wanted to reinforce that concept.

Speiser: What qualities did you say Dr. Nogueira possessed to make all this to happen? I know that people who will be reading this are going to say, "All right. If I want to start a writing center, what kinds of things do I have to look for?" Without administrative support, you're just not going to have a writing center.

Farrell: I've shared the following with Dr. Nogueira. When you and I were working on the NCTE workshop in Denver, and the year before when I presented in Washington, I had said, "In order to get a writing center started, you have to make your administration realize that what you are going to do is going to make them look good, too." The fact is that whatever is done in the school that makes the school look good also makes the administration look good. You want things that are effective, things that do encourage student and faculty growth and. . . .

Speiser: Learning.

Farrell: Yes, learning itself. I think that the key ingredient I found with our particular principal is that he is a reader. He keeps up with everything that is going on in education, so when I proposed the writing center, he was well aware of the fact that the future was heading towards improvement in writing skills. He was well aware of writing across the curriculum and how the writing center could function in that capacity. I think that those characteristics really helped him see the importance of the writing center within the scheme of the whole school.

Speiser: It's so important because, again, you were fortunate to work with someone who was aware of current research in writing. In fact, that's step one—writing center directors must get relevant information to the appropriate administrators. It may take a year or two to feed the information to them—get them fully aware of current research—so that when a proposal for a writing center comes around, they know something about it. It's not a shot in the dark; it counters the difficulties that occur, for example, the cost effectiveness of the writing center.

Farrell: Right. I think that the advantage people starting out today have is, hopefully, the material in this book, plus articles written in the *English Journal* and *Writing Lab Newsletter* on high school writing centers. When you and I started our programs, there just weren't articles or periodicals that spoke about high school writing centers. Nobody knew much about them. The first writing center that I found from my survey was one started in 1976, an isolated case that nobody else knew about. Today, there are over one hundred high school writing centers that people are aware of, ones that you can go visit. Heck, when we started, there weren't any to visit. If you went to see a college writing center, it was a whole different ball game. It was in a separate building; there weren't any bells ringing; students could stay until they finished something; they could come in the evening or the daytime; the time factor was entirely different; the staffing was different; and staff was dealing with mature students. It was hard to relate to what we had to do because we had to get material on college writing centers and adapt it.

Speiser: That's right.

Farrell: Now it's easier to start one, and I think the other thing is that you can always find *in the directory in the back of this book* names of existing high school writing centers. If you live in Ohio, for instance, there are three or four people that you can contact; that's going to save you hours and hours of time that we had to spend on just trying to figure out how the heck we were going to make a writing center work.

Speiser: I think the structure of the traditional American high school causes more difficulty than anything else. It makes the separation between a college writing center and a high school one obvious. Colleges provide more flexibility for their students. They aren't interested in whether a student is in a study hall or not.

Farrell: You need to write ten passes!

Speiser: That atmosphere! All of the paperwork that's involved in a high school that is not involved in a college makes it more difficult to make a high school writing center work. Initially,

Rumson-Fair Haven functioned like a college campus. There were no study halls.

Farrell: Right, you had all that unstructured time.

Speiser: *Lots* of unstructured time, so it lent itself to a writing center. Since that time, structure has been imposed, and that has caused difficulties.

Farrell: Yes, tell me about them.

Speiser: After a year of operation, our writing center was eliminated. However, the next year a group came in to evaluate the English department, and they asked, "What happened to the writing center?" Like magic, the writing center was resurrected under a new name: "writing lab." Then, after a year of operation, that, too. . . .

Farrell: Wait a minute. Let's back up a second. You had been given a summer grant to do research on setting up the writing lab, correct? The school invested money during the summer for you to open something new?

Speiser: Reopen.

Farrell: Reopen only under the name of writing lab, and then, after a year, it disappeared?

Speiser: Yes. Let me put things into perspective. After having a writing center for a year, I was learning, as I still am, about how writing centers work. What I saw was a nice, informal place for people to come to talk about their writing assignments and find out what they could do to improve their writing. My year-end goal was to evaluate where we were, do some more research, and then talk to the administration about expanding the writing center into one with a cross-curricular focus and interdisciplinary staff. Well, that didn't occur because there was a change in administration, and the new educational hierarchy felt that four classes plus the writing center was not acceptable. They felt that the students would be better served if the teacher were in the classroom teaching—"teaching," as James Britton would humorously describe it, being the art of dispensing knowledge "from the jug to the mug, pouring knowledge into students' heads." So, goodbye writing center.

Now, the group that I mentioned earlier, who came to evaluate the school, recommended that the writing center be reinstituted. They had done their homework, and they saw that it was a significant asset. Well, armed with their report and a summer grant to work out the mechanics, our writing center was born again. Although the summer grant only involved one of the instructors, it certainly helped because the philosophy and the processes, the nuts and bolts of the new writing center, were established. In September, the writing center was reinstituted under a new name, "the writing lab." I was directed to call it a lab.

Farrell: This is a good point at which to bring up the distinction that you found between the terms "center" and "lab."

Speiser: A writing center is a place where writing is honored. It's a center for thinking and learning with all the connotations of humanism and inquiry. A lab conjures up visions of a Frankensteinian place where people are dissected and SRA kits come out to be drilled and redrilled ad nauseam. It reminds me of a Band-Aid station, as you would say, Pam, for folks having problems, a remedial place. I'm not sure, but I think that's what some might have envisioned.

Farrell: Do you think the introduction of the high school proficiency test with a writing sample had something to do with the name change?

Speiser: I'm sure it did. The administration might have reasoned, "We've got to make sure we do very well on this state testing, and to do that, we are going to have this lab." If this was what the administration was thinking, however, it was never realized, for the writing lab turned out to be something quite different. Philosophically, the new lab was a place where students wrote as a way of learning to write; where there was a commitment to individualized instruction through conference teaching and tutoring; where there was a commitment to teach writing as a process; and where there was a major commitment to foster a confidence by focusing on learning rather than grading. The lab put the teaching of writing, the control of writing, and the responsibility for writing back into the hands of students by giving them a place and some space to talk about ideas, and to engage in the trial and error process of composing.

Farrell: So what happened?

Speiser: In essence, what happened was that, at the end of the school year, the administration decided there would no longer be a writing lab. This is something that will have to be faced by people who are going to put together writing labs/centers. A writing lab/center will be eliminated if administrators and Boards of Education are not convinced that it's okay for an instructor to tutor one to three students per class period. A writing lab/center will be eliminated if administrators and Boards of Education are not convinced that tutorials are the finest way to effect the improvement of thinking and writing.

Farrell: Now that you have mentioned the administration again, I have to bring up another point. At the time we started our programs years ago, you were supervisor of English while I was a classroom English teacher with five sections of English to teach each day. I had very little support from my supervisor, but I did have a very supportive principal. I set up the writing center as a writing-across-the-curriculum facility. I know there will be many people reading this book who will say, "I don't know anyone who will support me. What am I going to do?" Well, we both found that outside consultants coming to the school help because, first of all, we all know that anyone within the school itself cannot be an expert. You bring in paid consultants who live at least twenty-five miles away and they know something; that's a reality. But realistically, a consultant can present the research that you already know and make others aware and supportive of your ideas. That can make a big difference. [*The directory in the back of this book will help someone starting a writing lab/center find consultants to explain how their labs/centers work.*]

Speiser: Now Teacher Farrell has done the research, has read this and other works on writing centers, is convinced that a writing center is essential, but is having problems getting started. Teacher Farrell gets a consultant to talk about writing centers to the administration and the English department.

Farrell: And the consultant does such a good job that the administration is convinced.

Speiser: That's one way to do it. What about the administrators who are not in favor of a writing center? We've got to get them literature to read.

Farrell: Another thing to do—I know we've both done it—is make a point of gathering papers that students have worked on with writing center assistance and present those materials to the Board of Education. The students and I posted winning essays, entries in contests, college application essays, poetry and writing projects across the curriculum. We also gave demonstrations on the use of the word processors for writing, as part of the inservice programs. In other words, we have tried to keep the Board of Education and staff aware of what we're doing. As you mentioned before, if they and the community know what's going on, they're going to support it. I was very fortunate one year to have a parent who had just moved into the area volunteer one hour per week of her time. She didn't work with many students, but she read every book on writing that I had in the writing center. She also spoke to other parents about the writing center, and she was there at the board meetings. That was very positive.

Speiser: Maybe that's the best approach. First, do your homework, read this book, read other books, understand more about the composing process, and then get started. There must be some time during the school day that can be sacrificed so that you can start a writing lab/center. Do you have a study hall or professional period? Guess what—all you need is a peaceful place and public relations to get started.

Farrell: Let's add one thing. You've got to have a writing lab/center philosophy so clear in your own mind that you believe it down to the tips of your toes. I refer to it as being clearly embedded in my soul because, if it hadn't been, every wall I had run into along the way would have just destroyed me. The writing center never would have gotten off the ground.

Speiser: Give me an example of a wall.

Farrell: Okay. "We don't have anybody for released time. We can't let you work in the writing center." That's why I began to use peer tutors; I didn't have another body to put in the area. When I got a room the second year, I needed people to be in the room other than during my lunch period. I couldn't ask teachers to give up their lunch periods.

Speiser: You were able to get some students. . . .

Farrell: Because teachers were covering cafeteria supervision, library supervision, hall duty, study hall duty, whatever—there were no extra people. I was given writing center duty instead of cafeteria duty, so I was assigned there one period out of a full eight-period day. That's why being in the media center helped; there was a teacher assigned there every period, plus a librarian. That meant that students could be in the writing center because it was located within a larger room, the media center, which was already supervised.

Speiser: That's how we overcame some of our walls. Many high schools thrive on body counts; someone says students must be somewhere every second of the school day. This kind of makes me boil a little bit because physical accountability (hall passes, library passes, late passes) takes precedence over teaching and learning.

Farrell: It's another reality.

Speiser: A sad reality, sometimes.

Farrell: Yes, so for insurance purposes, the area had to be supervised, and I had to find a way to staff the writing center.

Speiser: What you're saying is whoever is going to read this book will do whatever it takes to get the lab/center going. We're not talking about where it is located (although that's a consideration, too), but we are talking about using the available resources. In your case, the available resources were students because there were no other resources available. At one point, I was fortunate enough to have teachers work there. That was great. Maybe, in a third school, there might be students who won't be available; teachers won't be available. Maybe they'll use community people. Whatever the situation, you need somebody—somebody who's trained—somebody who understands the writing process and is willing and able to operate as a tutor.

Farrell: You've got to know that you're going to run into brick walls. There's no way of getting around them. You were closed down, you started back up. You were closed down again. . . .

Speiser: And we'll start up again.

Farrell: Remember the Shmoo in *Li'l Abner*? You knock it over, it bounces back up. Donald Murray, Peter Elbow—you know the people I'm talking about—strongly influenced our thinking in setting up our writing centers. Without their ideas and that reinforcement, we probably wouldn't have done it.

What we can say to people who are trying to start a writing center is, "Okay, what do you do? You have this great philosophy of your own, you work with your own situation, but you also prepare yourself." Every state has some kind of a writing project course to attend that prepares you to teach writing. There are wonderful summer writing institutes at Bread Loaf or Northeastern University at Martha's Vineyard. Programs like these are available throughout the country for teachers who are interested in learning more about teaching writing. Those teachers are important for one very essential reason, and that is to provide you with a built-in support group to help you get your own program off the ground. Also, as one of my friends told me, she needed the arm of our Martha's Vineyard group because no one else in her own school system understood what she was trying to do. She just needed some positive reinforcement from one of the members of the network. That's what happens; you need it, and it's important. You can prepare yourself, and once you open your lab/center, you don't stop doing these things. You never stop. I mean, you and I have gone to how many conferences and presentations since 1981 and we still have problems with our labs/centers that we want to ameliorate. We're not going to get the problems resolved if we don't keep going to conferences and listening. I need a dose of some kind of writing workshop every six months just to keep up on what's going on and to try new methods. That's really important.

There's one other element that we haven't emphasized enough. It's the students. If it weren't for them, forget it.

Speiser: You're right, because that's why we're there in the first place, and they're the ones that make a writing center work because they come back with the information that says, "Guess what? I think I understand a little bit more about how I write, and I like this. I want to return. I want to come back and see you and talk to you about writing."

Farrell: After they graduate, too. That's what is interesting. They come back and, whether they've gone to college, vocational school, or work, these kids return and talk to you about the importance of the writing center.

Speiser: That's certainly proof enough for us, but it is even more important that "schools"—administrators, teachers, parents— see that writing is important. And one way to make schools aware is through a schoolwide study of writing.

Farrell: Yes, that's what we did. In both of our schoolwide writing-across-the-curriculum surveys, we studied the kinds of writing our students were doing in their classes. We learned that there needed to be a center, a place that could be the focus of writing.

Speiser: That's true. My survey indicated that the purposes, kinds, and amounts of writing were much too dependent upon individual teachers. I also inferred that optimum writing came from classrooms conducted by teachers who were trained to teach writing. They were more aware of the functions of writing and how writing could be used as a tool to learn, as well as a means of evaluation. It was clear that one way to improve schoolwide writing was to create a center and staff it with trained *writing* teachers.

Farrell: We were both looking at Britton's transactional, expressive, and poetic modes of writing in our surveys. Because most of the writing fell into only one of those categories, we became aware of the need for more variety of writing in order to think, to know, and to learn.

Speiser: Right. Maybe that's another way to get a writing center started. Be a little manipulative. Think, "I want a writing center. I'll take a survey and find out something that I suspect anyway—that there is insufficient writing in the transactional mode or in the expressive mode or there is insufficient writing across the curriculum." I'm going to meet some opposition, so I'll get some other people who are interested in writing and tell others, "I want to find out what kinds of things students write about now." Use trade-offs: "If you let me know what kinds of writing are going on, let me see the actual pieces, then I'll try to help you with a concern you have."

Farrell: You said "manipulative," and I'm sitting here saying to myself, "Well, I was manipulative; there's nothing wrong with that." My proposal was part of my M.A. in writing at Northeastern University. I proposed the writing center for one of my courses. That made it easier to say to my principal, "I'm doing this for a course." Sometimes that helps. By conducting surveys or researching for courses, or writing projects, you may get the administrative support you need.

Speiser: And how about computers? They were hot items, right? Do you remember when every student was going to become computer literate, and there was a shark frenzy of purchase orders to get more computers than the neighboring district?

Farrell: Sure. Then people realized that computer literacy wasn't what they thought it was. Many of the students had computers at home or didn't need all this training in computer programming.

Speiser: And as a result, there was a barrel of rotting Apples—too bad! This is a great situation if you want to start a writing center. I guess it's our moral sense that makes us shy away from the word "manipulative" because we don't like it.

Farrell: But a writing center is something positive that can't do anything but help the school. If you have to manipulate, do so. And remember, some districts are lucky. An Ohio superintendent has publicly stated that by next year, he wants all the high schools in the district to have writing centers.

Speiser: That's an enviable circumstance, but I know that there are districts oblivious to the need for a writing center. Either way, be sure to do your homework first. Don's use a writing center as a Band-Aid for a problem an administrator has. For example, if the statewide writing test scores are not high enough, the administration might say, "Next year's educational objectives will include the implementation of a new learning facility to enhance written communication skills."

Farrell: Translation—"We've got to bring up the scores on the statewide writing tests fast. We'll create a space where the failures will get remedial help. We'll let Speiser buy a couple of drill-and-kill software packages and tell him to solve the problem!"

Speiser: That's what they'll do. And they'll tell me to transform these students, who are totally turned off to writing and learning for a lot of other reasons, into scholars within a year. I'll accept this absurd challenge but then manipulate it. I'll turn the writing lab around so that it meets the needs of the students.

Farrell: And meeting the needs of students means creating a low-risk, positive environment that encourages dialogue or collaboration. No matter why students come to the writing lab or writing center, they need to know that it's okay to talk about their writing and talk about what they might be planning to write. We never had that in high school or college; we didn't have anyone to listen to what we were writing about during the writing process. It's very important for all of us to have that. Professional writers have other writers that they send their work to or call to ask, "How does this sound?" They know that collaboration is important. They know it's important to have another listener, another voice, involved in the whole writing process. We all need those listeners and those questions to help keep us on task and to help keep us moving forward.

Speiser: You're absolutely right. And one more thing. Don't forget evaluation. Be wise and set up approved evaluation tools before the center opens so that you won't be expected to do the impossible.

Farrell: Like tutor fifty students per day when you only have staff to handle sixteen.

Speiser: Exactly. And be sure to include a survey that measures attitudinal changes toward writing. In all cases, your evaluation should involve something besides a head count or points on statewide writing tests.

Farrell: I agree.

Speiser: And there's something else. A writing lab/center should not be a people dump. It should not be a place where Ms. Nevabend can send Butch Doe, her classroom nemesis. Don't buy that one. And don't let it become a proofreading service or a place where tutors write papers for students. A sound and clearly disseminated writing lab/center philosophy should mitigate these traps.

Farrell: Right. Finally, it should be a reinforcement of what's going on in the classrooms throughout the high school.

3 Goals and Philosophies of High School Writing Centers

Amy K. Levin
Scarsdale High School
Scarsdale, New York

High school writing centers tend, out of necessity, to be pragmatic institutions. Their offerings and facilities are often determined by such practicalities as the available space or the timing of the director's free periods—not by carefully researched and developed philosophies. Stephen North's assessment of the proliferation of college writing centers is even more appropriate to the centers in high schools:

> The speed of this growth, unfortunately, has enabled writing center staffs to do little more than survive, to do what they can to improve the lot of the writers in their charge, leaving precious little time, money, or energy for research into the hows and whys of their operations. (North 1984, 25)

As late arrivals in high schools that already suffer from decreased funding for established programs, writing centers face a continual struggle for their very existence; as a result, writing centers may fail to fulfill many of their original philosophical objectives. One center, for instance, has been operating informally in a planning stage since 1982, without ever becoming an official part of the school system.

Nevertheless, the very existence and growth in number of high school writing centers at the national level indicate that a certain philosophy is at work. This philosophy is largely the same whether a center is staffed by students, like most of those discussed in this article, or by teachers. Both types of centers assist individuals at various stages of the writing process in a low-risk environment. Those with peer tutors also promote certain relationships among students; those staffed by teachers model informal relationships between adolescents and adults. In any case, the spread of both types of writing centers suggests that, although the centers may be competing for limited resources within school districts, they do fit into certain institutional goals.

Current literature on writing centers, such as Gary Olson's collection of articles, *Writing Centers: Theory and Administration* (1984), or Steward's and Croft's excellent practical work, *The Writing Laboratory: Organization, Management, and Methods* (1982), discusses writing center philosophies primarily in student terms and concentrates on college centers. Olson's collection of articles, for instance, deals with cognitive skill development and audience awareness. Yet institutional objectives, which are critical, often receive short shrift. A writing center director, especially in a high school, ignores institutional goals at his or her own peril. When a center is constantly fighting for survival, it must be able to justify itself regularly, not only as it affects small groups, but also as it affects the structure of the entire school. Realism (and politics) takes precedence over idealism on this point; supervisors and administrators tend to think in global terms.

Institutional and writing center objectives both include providing individual assistance for under-represented populations. These populations vary from school to school: they may include advanced placement students, ESL students, remedial students, or so-called average or regular students who are neglected because the proverbial squeaky wheel gets the grease. At Scarsdale High School, the writing center's greatest successes have been with students from such groups. We have helped tenth-grade honors students with their research papers—who says honors students never need help?—and we have scheduled weekly meetings with several ESL students. For one Korean student, a year's work in the writing center included opportunities to converse as well as to write. His tutor was excited by his progress:

> He used to be very quiet and shy. Over the months, he has become more open and talkative. We talk about various things, such as the senior class play, SATs, etc. He talks openly to me now without the reserve he used to have. We have been writing papers for social studies. . . .

At Scarsdale, the writing center has also attracted a number of students from regular level classes who want a little extra help or encouragement with their writing. Unlike some other writing centers, ours has seen few remedial students—and this has been important. We are aware that students often stigmatize remedial facilities; and we want to avoid a situation in which we attract so many remedial students that others perceive the center as a facility available only to them. Similarly, James Upton of Burlington (Iowa) Community High School has discussed the importance of making a writing center a place for *all* students:

We also changed the name of the proposed center to avoid the often unfair connotation of a writing lab as a place where lower ability or "dumb" students were sent to catch up.

At the same time, however, to the extent that a center may offer remediation, it can also help fill a second important institutional goal, especially in states with required competency tests. A writing center can offer tutorial assistance for students who need to pass such exams in order to graduate.

Districts with writing-across-the-curriculum programs benefit from writing centers, too, because the centers deal with writing in all disciplines. In addition, writing centers may encourage students to publish and distribute their work, whether they have written poetry, scientific studies, or interviews with other students. Thus, the existence of a writing center is proof of the importance placed on writing skills by a school district.

On a less academic level, writing centers that employ peer tutors can model certain relationships among students that administrators might well wish to foster. First, by offering peer tutoring, writing centers can reach students who are not comfortable with adults; the setting poses few risks for such youngsters. Second, such centers promote collaborative, noncompetitive relationships among students; instead of challenging each other for grades, students in a writing center help each other. This goal may be especially important in districts with a high percentage of college-bound students, where the pressure to excel may be intense. A tutor from Scarsdale was particularly positive about the personal rewards of tutoring:

> The most rewarding activity in which I participate is the Writing Center. . . . My work in the Writing Center offers me not only the satisfaction of helping others, but also an opportunity to enrich myself academically and emotionally.

Last but not least, a writing center, as a primarily student-operated concern, is relatively inexpensive for a school district. Although many centers have sophisticated equipment, including computers, tape recorders, and filmstrip projectors, others contain only the most basic necessities: tables, chairs, paper, a dictionary, a thesaurus. In a time of tight school budgets, a crucial part of a writing center's philosophy may indeed be to provide assistance and enrichment in writing at the lowest possible cost.

The goals discussed thus far have been practical and institutionally oriented. But the philosophy of a writing center as it affects students is also important, for the center can benefit both tutors and their student clients.

Tutors learn about the writing process by intervening frequently in the writing of others. At the very least, most of the tutors are competent writers, students who have learned the advantages of working through various stages of the writing process. But the common notion that a skill is fully mastered only when one has to teach it holds true. As Harriet Marcus (1984, 66) has stated in an *English Journal* article, "We believe that in teaching others, we learn best and we hoped our peer tutors' involvement in the center would improve their already competent writing as they gained awareness about writing and themselves." As an observer removed from the piece of writing, a tutor can see why a revision or an extended brainstorming session can help. In addition, tutors learn about the variations in individual writing processes.

Two of the most essential skills for tutors are careful listening and critical reading. In the writing center, both abilities must be developed. Tutors are expected to read or hear drafts of essays, and they must immediately respond to the compositions. The editing skills that tutors gain in these situations are ultimately useful with their own writing.

Working in a writing center helps tutors not only with their own writing (and their college applications), but also with their interpersonal skills. The tutors at Scarsdale, for instance, have to work with everyone from reluctant remedial students to timid freshmen, from touchy advanced placement candidates to non-English-speaking youngsters. By observing someone's difficulties and by collaborating with students from various groups within the school, tutors gain respect for the diversity of others. In her journal, one of my students, who was successful academically and socially, recorded her experience with a troubled ninth grader. On one of the ninth grader's first visits, the tutor noted:

> [This student] came to the center with no books, paper or pen. She had no idea why she was there. I explained to her my position in helping her, what the center does, what we will be doing in the sessions, etc. She seemed totally uninterested and like it was a waste of time. I can honestly say that I am not looking forward to helping her with her bad attitude. But I am going to try as hard as I can to spark some interest and enthusiasm in her and hopefully help her. We'll see!

After a more successful session three weeks later, in which the ninth grader was able to write and revise a paragraph, the tutor commented that both girls felt more satisfied:

> She left pretty happy, knowing that now she didn't have to do the assignment at home. I thought the session went well and that we got a lot accomplished.

Tutoring in difficult situations, such as the preceding one, also gives tutors more empathy for their own teachers. One senior kept commiserating with the teacher of a particularly difficult class!

Writing center work provides tutors with a final, very important advantage—self-confidence. Often, tutors are able students academically, but may not be "stars" in the social or athletic worlds of their peers. At the writing center, they not only receive attention and assistance from the director, but also gain the respect and admiration of fellow students. One tutor recounted the end of a session with a junior:

> I gave him some solid assistance, but he came up with much of it [an introduction] himself with my prodding. He left exclaiming, "That's amazing. You're a senior, right?" He obviously felt confident and appreciative—and *I* felt *AWESOME!*

The exhilaration of the tutor and the other student in this case reminds us that the tutors are not the only students who benefit from the collaborative setting of a writing center. Like the tutors, students will gain a heightened sense of the writing process given time and a place to work through assignments step-by-step with another person. And although, ideally, classroom teachers provide such assistance, in reality, they are often unable to do so. Steward and Croft address this goal of writing centers in their section on philosophy:

> A philosophical commitment to individualization through conference teaching is the one tenet fundamental to all of the most successful writing laboratories that we have surveyed. This belief means also the commitment to process, for laboratories can emphasize the writing process as classrooms, no matter how organized, seldom can. (1982, 5)

This point is even truer in high schools than in colleges because a teacher in a high school may be instructing over one hundred students in composition, in addition to having lunchroom duty, study hall, and sundry other chores.

Moreover, precisely because tutors are *not* classroom teachers, they often can step back and encourage their peers to apply what they have learned. That is, rather than correcting or fixing errors, a good tutor will show a student how to make changes. Thus the clients of writing centers will learn how to think and edit independently, in preparation for college essay writing. Cognitive development is promoted as writing skills are enhanced.

It is also important for students to have an audience for their work before it is graded. Students may be encouraged to take risks with their writing and to see that criticism need not be a purely negative activity. As students watch and hear others react to their writing, they gain a stronger sense of audience; as they hear tutors relate their own experiences with similar writing problems, they develop an awareness that they are part of a community of writers. Finally, students achieve a necessary realization that "it can be done"—by talking to peer tutors, they learn that the assignments which give them heartaches or anxiety have been survived by others.

Although many of the same experiences may be found in centers staffed by teachers or other adult professionals, such centers have their own advantages, too. First, students may develop closer relationships with adults in the informal setting of the writing center; they may be less defensive about criticism when it is offered in a low-risk setting with no grades involved. In addition, as students who work with tutors see adults struggling, for example, with phrasing or organization, they realize that writing is a common endeavor and a difficult task for everyone. Students understand that their problems with writing are not a mark of their stupidity or incompetence but a normal, even predictable, circumstance.

In addition to sharing a number of common goals, individual writing centers, whether staffed by adults or students, also have specific aims appropriate to their schools' needs. Some writing centers, such as the one at Red Bank Regional High School, in Little Silver, New Jersey, work extensively with word processing. The center has a library of software to help students with the writing process and their writing skills, and students may come in to work on papers alone as well as with tutors. The same writing center also keeps a file of competitions. In Scarsdale, where a number of students seek help with research papers, we have found it necessary for tutors to have expertise in methods of documentation and a familiarity with library resources. In contrast, the center at Mount Markham Senior High School in West Winfield, New York, has worked with students in danger of failing. The particular goals of writing centers are as different as their schools, although one variation exists in several districts—writing centers serve as a liaison between a district and a local college. Students at Red Bank Regional High School work closely with and train with students from Monmouth College. This association contributes to the tutors' sense of professionalism and gives the college a heightened presence in the community.

Varied as writing center goals and philosophical tenets may be, the director of a writing center must remember the most fundamental point—a good writing center will have as its philosophy living up to its name. It will aim at making writing central in the school and in students' lives by involving students and adults in a collaborative approach to writing. A writing center will foster a positive attitude toward writing and encourage students to feel more confident about engaging in the essentially human act of communication.

References

Marcus, Harriet. "The Writing Center: Peer Tutoring in a Supportive Setting." *English Journal* 73, no. 5 (September 1984): 66–67.

North, Stephen M. "Writing Center Research: Testing Our Assumptions." *Writing Centers: Theory and Administration,* 24–35.

Olson, Gary, ed. *Writing Centers: Theory and Administration.* Urbana, Ill.: NCTE, 1984.

Steward, Joyce, and Mary Croft. *The Writing Laboratory: Organization, Management, and Methods.* Glenview, Ill.: Scott, Foresman, 1982.

Other quotations come from surveys of writing center directors conducted by Pamela Farrell and from tutor reports and journals from the Scarsdale High School Writing Center, 1985-86. The seven tutors that year, all of whom were instrumental in developing the writing center's philosophy, were Wendy Brenner, Beverly Brown, David Ephron, Jolie Goldstein, James Kikkawa, Nicolas Meyer, and Andrew Schmolka.

4 Finding a Space

Richard Allen
Pamela B. Farrell
Red Bank Regional High School
Little Silver, New Jersey

In reading the responses to my survey of high school writing center directors, I noticed a pattern in the descriptions of facilities throughout the country. Therefore, I asked several directors to send sketches of their labs/centers. Those who responded had very similar layouts, so I asked industrial arts teacher Dick Allen to plot sketches on the computer. The resulting diagrams (see figures 1 through 5) show the tremendous similarities and offer you, the reader, a look at the actual space apportionments of existing high school writing labs/centers.

As important as the space itself might be, the location of the space may be even more important. Based on my survey, the most desirable or functional location is within or adjacent to the library or media center. Responses indicate that the reasons seem to be visibility, access, and necessity: public schools, by law, must provide supervision for every area within the school where students are permitted. Since most writing center directors also teach classes and since other professional staff cannot be released from assignments such as hall duty, facilities could not function during the entire school day. If, however, the writing lab/center is located within the media center, then a professional assigned to that area may be technically and legally responsible for the writing lab/center space as well. As mentioned in the chapters dealing with peer tutors, students rather than professional staff may maintain the lab/center during the periods when the director is teaching. In schools with full-time directors and professional staff, the proximity to the media center helps facilitate research and availability of audiovisual equipment and security.

The other area of the building that seems to be a viable location is the English area. Whether the school has a wing designated the "English wing" or there are open classrooms within one section of the school, many directors have found this location advantageous because of its convenience and accessibility. Teachers staffing the writing lab/center, mostly English teachers, need not travel around the school to get to their writing lab/center assignment. Also, students can easily be sent there from English classes with the knowledge that they will arrive before the class period ends! On a personal note, I have found this location best because all students have an English class and, therefore, pass by our open doors sometime during the school day. Many stop in just to see what the facility has to offer them, and, for some, a warm "hello" is the only positive experience they have had during their day. Therefore, many return on the premise of visiting when, in fact, they want to talk about their writing.

Other locations, for the most part, have been determined for the directors by administrators: in order to implement a writing lab/center, directors have willingly taken any available or converted space in the building just to "get their feet in the door." A writing lab/center cannot grow if it does not exist in the first place. If I had not accepted the file cabinet and round table to use under the steps in the media center, I never would have been given the locked room with a computer that we outgrew two years later. Now I have an adequate space, but I must share it with classes all day. Unfortunately, these anecdotal comments are some of the realities of space and location.

Many of the directors who have contributed to this book infer or even describe a certain atmosphere that must be maintained in their writing labs/centers. They refer to a "nonthreatening space" or what I have always called a "low-risk environment." Through the use of plants, carpeting, private corners, posters, and so forth, many directors have been able to create a comfortable area where students feel free to talk about writing, work on their own writing process, write to think, learn, and know. Certainly the personality of the director will influence this creation of space, but most directors insist on the input of students in the decorating of the area. Depending on the philosophy of the lab/center, the director and students must work on creating a friendly environment that encourages students to come there for remediation, enrichment, experimentation with language and ideas. Therefore, diagrams and locations cannot describe what is expressed in the thoughts and feelings of directors in depicting their own writing labs/centers.

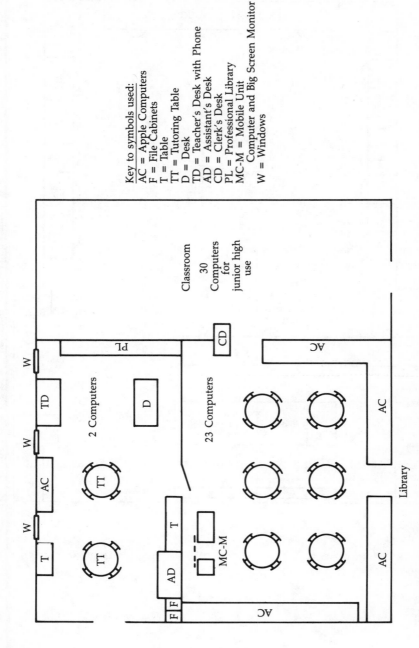

Fig. 1. Hazelwood West High School Writing Lab.

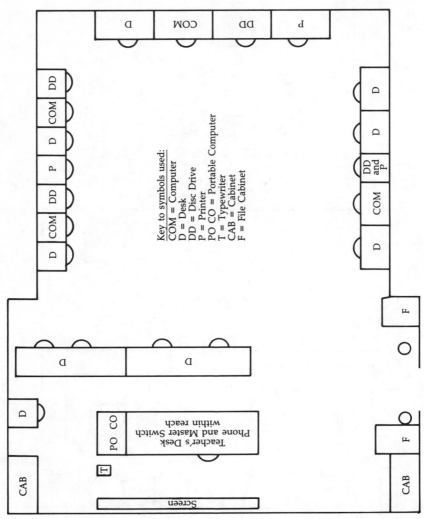

Key to symbols used:
COM = Computer
D = Desk
DD = Disc Drive
P = Printer
PO CO = Portable Computer
T = Typewriter
CAB = Cabinet
F = File Cabinet

Fig. 2. The Write Place, Mt. Lebanon Senior High School.

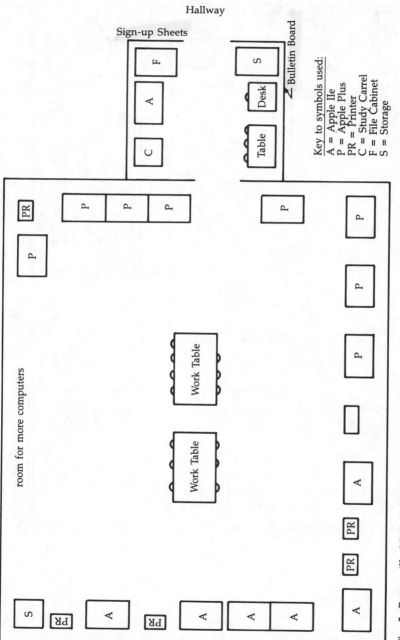

Fig. 3. Pattonville High School Writing Center.

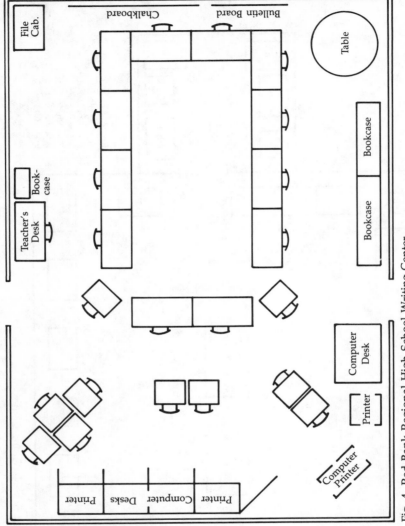

Fig. 4. Red Bank Regional High School Writing Center.

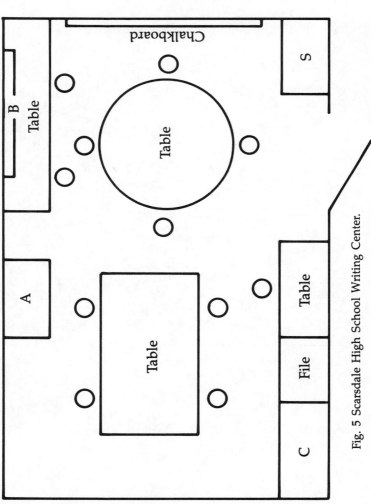

Key to symbols used:
A = Apple IIe
    and printer
B = Bookshelves
C = Study Carrell
S = Storage

Fig. 5 Scarsdale High School Writing Center.

5 Staffing the Writing Center

Harriet Marcus
Oak Knoll School
    of the Holy Child Jesus
Summit, New Jersey

Pamela B. Farrell
Red Bank Regional High School
Little Silver, New Jersey

Staffing by Peer Tutors

The Oak Knoll Writing Center has been in operation for six years, but contrary to general expectations, our writing center is not staffed by our school writing experts (the teachers); instead we staff our center exclusively with students. The 250 girls who attend the Upper School may use the writing center whenever they have unscheduled time, including before and after school, lunch period, or free time. A student may sign up on the writing center door to reserve a time slot in advance, or she may take her chances and drop in when she is free. A student may be required to go to the writing center by a teacher, or she may decide on her own to go for help. A student may bring a school essay with organizational problems, a short story without a dynamic beginning, or a poem in need of an audience. Over the years, the number of students using the writing center has steadily increased. Surveyed annually, our students endorse the peer-staffed center; they feel their sessions improve their writing because of the supportive and collaborative environment.

Our decision to use students, not teachers, as tutors was based on educational and practical considerations. Philosophically, we believe that peer tutors are powerful coaches for their fellow students. When a teacher says, "You know, I'm not sure what you're saying in this

The section devoted to staffing with peer tutors was written by Harriet Marcus; the section on staffing with faculty, by Pamela B. Farrell.

39

part of your essay," often students attribute this lack of understanding to a generation gap; but when a respected fellow student gives similar feedback, the client really concentrates. Our students listen to each other. From a practical standpoint, in our small, independent school, we need our talented students because our writing teachers are too busy. Not only do the teachers moderate the newspaper and literary magazine and help direct the school plays, but they also preside over the student council and the forensics club. We could not have staffed the center with our teachers; they were simply not available.

While we were convinced that, with training, peer tutors could be powerful writing coaches, we were concerned about how we could get our most talented student writers to give up two to three periods per week of their precious, unscheduled time to staff our center. We had no money to pay them; we couldn't promise them a lightened course load; we didn't have a luxurious setting with which to tempt them. The plan we finally devised works well for us. We *require* all of our junior and senior students who wish to be part of our honors or advanced placement English programs to be writing center tutors. This makes a lot of sense to us, for the students in our college-preparatory school who would want to participate in an advanced English program would need to be students who already display competence in writing. In our communication to interested juniors and seniors, we explain clearly that, aside from the standard requirements for acceptance into our honors or advanced placement programs (such as good grades in English, outstanding teacher recommendations, high verbal SAT scores, ability to do independent work, and enthusiasm for English), students need to commit themselves to a minimum of two, fifty-minute periods per week to work in the writing center. (Those students with no unscheduled school time can work in the center before or after school or during lunch periods—food is permitted in the center). Happily, this writing center tutoring requirement has in no way affected the number of students who apply to our honors or advanced placement programs; in fact, the number of applications has increased even with the added tutoring responsibility.

We have committed ourselves to student tutors, but what makes student tutors commit themselves to us? A writing center tutor is an admired and respected person at Oak Knoll. The tutors are proud to have been selected; they like the challenge of helping their friends and classmates improve their writing. In the required writing center journals, the tutors often note their feelings of competence:

> Jean came to me and asked me to go over her paper with her. It was a paper on Arthur Miller's *The Crucible*. She had good ideas

but she needed a little help organizing. We also corrected some awkward sentences and punctuation and spelling mistakes. She also asked me to help her with ideas for a conclusion which I did. Her paper was good and answered the question the teacher's assignment had asked. Since Jean and I are good friends, it was fun to work with her. She listens to me and I listen to her and together we get a lot accomplished. (Debbie M.)

This trimester was a *very* busy one for me, both academically and socially. I went through a lot of heartaches coupled with happy occasions and new challenges. Writing Center has been a major part of my life these past three months. Being late for class, taking papers home and missing out on my lunches and free time were all things that came with the responsibility of being a Writing Center tutor. When I applied and was accepted into English Honors, I had no idea my life would be such a confused whirlwind, but now, I wouldn't change a minute! I got to know many students, learned from their mistakes and made many new friends while balancing my time between pizza and a paper on *Tess of the D'Urbevilles*. I love having such a big commitment and responsibility and having to stick to it whether my life that day started off on the wrong foot or whether I came from an amazing party the night before. I feel so strongly about having the chance to help others while having fun and I hope I can continue doing so for more prospective Writing Center tutors in the years to come. (Carolina E.)

As an added incentive, writing center tutors are able to participate in our school service program. If they have accumulated the required number of service hours, they receive service credit that is noted on their permanent file.

The tutors are also made aware that, while they are helping other students improve their writing, their own writing improves as well. Many tutors have commented in their journals that they've noted strengths and weaknesses in their papers after they've worked with a student; in clarifying a concept for others, the coach learns it for herself:

I have tutored mainly seventh and eighth grade students this trimester. I found I enjoy tutoring this age group the most because they are the most open and least self conscious about their mistakes and problems. I've gotten to know a lot of girls through tutoring, but perhaps more importantly I have strengthened many of my skills. For example, when I discovered I had trouble explaining some of the punctuation errors students made, I decided to look the topics up in texts to clarify the rules in my mind. (Caragh N.)

In no way do writing center tutors feel that they are directive teachers imposing their will on pliant, helpless peers. What the tutors enjoy is the feeling of camaraderie and competence that the writing center fosters. Tutor and client actively participate in the learning process. They collaborate to solve problems, make decisions, and improve writing:

> When I tutor someone we usually have a set way of going about it. I first have her read her paper to me and then I ask her if she has a specific problem with it that she wants to work on. If not, we go paragraph by paragraph and discuss new ideas and errors. I haven't yet had a bad experience in Writing Center. I try my best to help the client improve her paper, but if for some reason I don't feel that she left with the best paper that she could have written, (which does sometimes happen because every paper isn't perfect) at least we made friends and she'll come back another time to try again. (Missy J.)

While Oak Knoll students (both tutors and clients) have benefited from the peer-staffed writing center, there are, of course, problems that arise when students provide the services. First, there is the concern about the nonempathetic tutor. Because we require all honors and advanced placement English students to tutor, we occasionally find a talented English student who, initially, may not possess the interpersonal skills necessary to be a sensitive tutor. This student needs additional attention during the training sessions, careful monitoring during her first writing center conferences, and continual feedback from the supervisor during the year. In fact, the training sessions and the monthly meetings for all tutors should focus, in part, on the importance of making students feel welcome in a nonauthoritarian, collaborative environment. Tutors should be encouraged to discuss the personal dimensions of their session, not just the problems they uncovered with deep structure and surface errors.

In addition to the nonempathetic peer tutor, there is the annoying problem of the no-show tutor. It is disappointing and frustrating for a student to arrive at the writing center for her appointment and find no one available to help her. When tutors know in advance that they are going to be absent, they are required to find another tutor to fill their time slot. This system usually works quite well. Occasionally a tutor will leave school ill and be unable to arrange for a substitute. This is when the supervisor, if available, substitutes for the absent tutor. Other supportive teachers can be called in at the last moment, as well. The best solution to the absent tutor problem is to schedule two or more tutors for the same time slot. This not only allows coverage when one tutor doesn't show up, but it also enables several students to receive tutoring at the same time.

Finally, there is the problem of the authoritarian tutor. Sometimes we discover that a tutor is acting as a directive teacher, pencil in hand, correcting mistakes for a client. We teach our tutors never to put a mark on a student's paper. Any changes agreed upon should be made by the tutee, who is, after all, learning not only how to revise this particular paper, but also how to revise, eventually on her own, any paper she writes. Tutors help students become their own best editors.

Since the tutors are admonished against doing the work for the client, why have one or more teachers report to the supervisor that they have suspected that a particular student's paper was more the effort of the tutor than the effort of the student? Peer pressure is the answer. Once in a while, a tutor finds it difficult to resist the entreaties of a student who claims she will fail her course if her paper (which she has put off until the last minute) is not superb. Couldn't the tutor, her friend, take the paper home and write some suggestions? Left unsolved, this problem could undermine the faculty's belief that, when a student uses the writing center, she collaborates on her writing, but she doesn't have her work done for her. The best way to combat this problem is to address it from the start during training sessions and to role-play face-saving techniques so that the tutors can firmly but gracefully extricate themselves from an uncomfortable (and dishonest) situation.

Knowing the problems in advance can help create a successful student-staffed writing center. Talented honors and advanced placement English students, well trained and well monitored, can make an excellent staff for a high school writing center. They are enthusiastic, responsible, and sensitive; they are eager to learn and to help their peers. Not too long ago, the English department chairperson of another independent school asked me how I could, in good conscience, sanction the idea of a center where students would do little else than pass on mistakes from one to another. I assured him that, while, on occasion, a surface error might not be spotted and ferreted out, on the whole, Oak Knoll's writing center fostered interaction between students in a supportive, nurturing environment where students came away with a positive attitude about work, while feeling they had improved the quantity and quality of their writing.

Staffing by Faculty

Many schools insist that the only way to staff an effective writing lab/center is by using trained professionals. Although I do not have that luxury, I more than agree that, if your administration permits, trained writing instructors should be released from class assignments to staff a writing lab/center. In the sections describing the training of such staff, directors discuss the advantages of using professionals in the writing facility. Naturally, the professionals staffing the facility must have a common philosophy and similar training in the teaching of writing. Nothing proves more ineffective than a group of professionals giving mixed instructions or directions to student writers. Therefore, staffing by professionals must include an isolated training program before the facility opens.

Many of the existing high school writing labs/centers have developed programs that have worked in conjunction with college facilities. Some, such as West High School, Central High School, and Kirkwood High School, have modeled their training of staff after nearby college or university writing centers. Others have staffed their facilities with teachers who have participated in a national writing project course. Hazelwood West High School and J. P. McCaskey High School are examples. Finally, several schools have worked out collaborative projects with colleges and universities. For instance, Logan High School and Utah State University exchange faculty as part of their writing lab/center work, and Kenmore High School and Akron University use student teachers as well as instructors in their collaboration.

From my survey, 31 percent of the high school writing labs/centers are staffed entirely by professionals. Though more are staffed by student tutors (41 percent), many (27 percent) function with a combination of professional and student tutors. The reason for the lack of full-time professional staff, on the basis of the survey, seems to be a lack of commitment on the part of the administration: most schools are not willing to give up one teacher per period to staff a writing lab/center because that would equal the salary of one full-time teacher. However, there are schools (31 percent) from the survey who have hired full-time writing lab/center directors, indicating that staffing by professionals is important to the success of the writing labs/centers in those schools.

How do these writing labs/centers function when staffed by professionals? In most cases, teachers are assigned to the facility in place of a classroom or extra duty. They help students in different ways, depending on the purpose of the individual facility. In 99 percent of the cases, the teachers do not grade the students on their work in the writing lab/center, nor do they correct papers for other teachers. They are there to function as readers/listeners, conference guides, coaches, counselors. With the correct training and philosophy to meet the goals of an individual writing lab/center, professional tutors offer students an opportunity to work with teachers in a much more pleasant, less threatening environment to encourage the improvement of student writing.

6 Scheduling

Barbara Brooks
Pattonville High School
Maryland Heights, Missouri

Carol Lefelt
Highland Park High School
Highland Park, New Jersey

Scheduling at Pattonville

Pattonville High School is a large (2,500 student population) middle class suburban school located in St. Louis County, Missouri. The school day has six periods of fifty-four minutes each, with optional zero and seventh hours. Our writing center began four years ago as the result of the initiative of a colleague who had become involved with the Gateway Writing Project. She was provided with one computer, one disk drive and a printer, and was scheduled a three-hour consecutive block of time in lieu of teaching classes. During this time, she trained student tutors, conferred with individual students, and gave presentations on writing in other content areas. The use of the computer allowed her to keep meticulous records of writing center activities, but conferences and presentations were always the main focus. Coincidentally, this happened at a point when our district was looking for ways to incorporate computers into our schools. Our department chair requested a lab for drill and practice, and thus we obtained nine Apple Plus computers.

With the support of the department chair and the supervising principal, the writing center was expanded to a full day of operation for the following year and moved to the room that housed the computers. The teacher who developed our program continued to have three consecutive hours in the center to direct and train new coaches. Three other teachers were assigned one-hour time slots for one semester

The first half of this chapter is composed by Barbara Brooks; the second, by Carol Lefelt.

as part of their teaching schedule. At the end of the semester, three more teachers were assigned one-hour time slots. This meant that the director taught only two classes and the other writing coaches, who had one hour each of center time, taught four classes. Since no students are assigned to the center per se, the coaches were free to confer with students, prepare and give presentations, learn various computer programs, and build activities files.

Admittedly, this released time from assigned classes increased the class size for everybody. Our large department of some twenty teachers made staffing the center a delicate and often fiery ordeal. Some of our colleagues saw the opening of the writing center as an opportunity to obtain a "cushy" schedule and felt that we should immediately set up a seniority-based rotating list for scheduling. Others believed that teacher training and experience in writing should be our criteria. For years, we had an elective curriculum where many teachers had not formally taught writing. For example, one teacher might teach five sections of filmmaking, or three sections of advanced reading and two sections of "Preparing for the Future," none of which focuses on the writing process. Some colleagues argued that all English teachers know how to teach writing even if they have taught five hours of the same elective each day for four years straight.

Teaching assignments are made by the department chair, who first solicits our input. Final approval of all schedules, however, is given by our supervising principal. Because of the uproar over the staffing and directing of the writing center, it soon became apparent that guidelines needed to be set and followed. The major problem centered on the disagreement about the need for actual course work in teaching writing and experience in teaching writing as a process. We never did come up with total agreement on the guidelines and probably never will.

Another problem occurred at the end of the year when our director resigned. Our solution was to once again change the staffing. Now we have two teachers serving as codirectors, who each have a two-hour consecutive block of center time for the entire year and who also teach three classes. Two other teachers have one hour each and teach four classes, with staff changing at the semester's end. Thus, four new coaches are used each year. This was also the year we added five Apple IIe computers and three printers.

Our present plan of codirectors having two hours each of center time has been very effective. Now in our third year of operation, we have a writing center equipped with nineteen computers and five printers and we service almost 200 students per month in addition to preparing and giving presentations. Although we have added responsibilities because of the computer equipment, our philosophy hasn't changed. We still place a high priority on student conferences. The difference is that, now, when conferencing, a writing coach can expect to also be interrupted by the six or so students who are word processing as they need help revising and printing. Our connection with the computers has also resulted in teachers signing up their whole class for several days at a time. The disadvantage is that it is difficult for one writing coach to supervise eighteen students; the one-on-one conference time is lost. However, when whole classes come, we get several of them "hooked" on the ease of revising with computers, and they make return visits on their own so that they can get more individualized help.

Student Scheduling

To ensure an appointment, students are asked to use the sign-up sheets posted outside the center door. Separate sign-up sheets are displayed; one for a conference and one for independent work. Some of the independent work involves using various programs such as Print Shop, Newsroom, drill and practice exercises, SAT review, and word processing. The sheet provides for six hours and each hour is divided into approximately fifteen-minute time blocks for conferences. Students are allowed to sign up for the entire hour if they feel that it is necessary.

Even though the sign-up sheets are always posted a week in advance, we get a lot of drop-in business. Nevertheless, we insist that, before students arrive for their scheduled time or their drop-in visit, they report to the teacher whose class they will be missing and ask for permission to attend the center. We have passes made up for this purpose, and we always see to it that the teacher receives notification of the student's visit. Students coming for conferences are encouraged to submit rough drafts at least one day ahead of time so that the coach can be familiar with the writing. Usually, they come to the visit with assignment in hand. Bringing the necessary materials with them, such as the actual writing assignment, primary source or resource notes, and any prewriting already done in class, is very helpful.

Teachers may urge a student to use the writing center, but the final decision is always with the student.

Teacher Scheduling

We keep a master plan book in the writing center to record teacher requests for classroom presentation and for word-processing instruction. We prefer to have at least one week's notice on presentations, especially if they involve lesson designing with the teacher (see chapter 20.) Teachers may also sign up their entire class for a visit. We have several story starter programs that we use to introduce students to word processing. Frequently, a teacher sends half the class on one day, and the other half the following day.

This year, the teachers of the junior/senior writing class used word processing to teach revision. Since there are ten sections of this class and the average class size is twenty-eight students, with some classes having as many as thirty-four, they needed to block out three weeks of time just to accommodate the large numbers. In the future, we intend to schedule these classes for no more than one week at a time, with a week off to allow for conferences, which are still our highest priority.

The growth of our writing center in just three years has been phenomenal. We still struggle with the view of some colleagues that we have an easy schedule, but we continually see an increase in the number of other content area teachers who realize the value of our assistance in designing writing assignments to suit their needs. We also have the enthusiastic support of teachers allowing students to visit the center during their class time, even if the assignment is not for their class. And nothing compares with the warm feeling that comes when a student stops by to say, "I just wanted to tell you I got an 'A' on that paper you helped me with. Thanks for your help. I'll be back here with the next paper."

Scheduling at Highland Park

Highland Park High School is a small New Jersey suburban school of about 700 students ranging from grades 8–12. Our writing center, which is staffed by students from grades 10–12, started operation in 1984 in a tiny windowless room in the school library, where the librarians function as supervisors of a sort—because of insurance requirements and because, as writing center advisor, I also teach four periods per day and am not always in the library. We have since moved out of the airless cubicle and occupy a larger space in the rear of the library, near the large windows overlooking the athletic fields.

Students are trained to be peer tutors in a class called "Writing and Responding," which meets three times per week during the school day and counts for three credits. The course requires that tutors spend at least one period per week staffing the writing center. Scheduling time for these tutors to be in the writing center and making sure they are indeed there at those times are two of my biggest headaches at the start of the school year.

There are always two groups of tutors in September: those trained the previous year, who are ready to open the writing center and begin tutoring around October 1, and those newly enrolled in Writing and Responding, who will be ready to start tutoring sometime after Thanksgiving. (Last year we started with nine tutors and added nine more on January 6. This year we started with nine tutors and added fifteen on December 1.)

Experienced Tutors

I require the experienced tutors to meet with me as a group twice per month—and here is my first scheduling problem. It has become clear after long hassles that the only workable solution is to meet from 4:00 to 6:00 or 5:00 to 7:00 on a particular weekday night, every other week. Otherwise, we could never find a time after school when everyone would be available, for these students not only participate in every other imaginable school activity, but also have after-school jobs or other commitments. To my surprise, each year the tutors readily agree to the late hour and rarely miss meetings. In fact, these evening meetings are quite productive and fun, probably because they occur outside the school day. Sometimes we bring in snacks or supper and stay later when necessary without worrying about running into the time reserved for other activities.

I usually wait to publish a writing center schedule until the end of September, when students' individual schedules are fairly set; at this time they know when they have band practice, rotating choir, student council, yearbook, science labs, and so on and so forth. (We have lots of discussions about the possibility of "over-commitment.")

I call our first evening session sometime in early September, maybe during the second week of school. At this time I do the following:

1. Distribute independent study forms that students must submit to the guidance department and a list of requirements they must fulfill in order to receive independent study credit. Students rarely tutor just to receive these one or two independent study credits (they receive one credit per year for each period per week they spend tutoring for the whole year). I insist on this arrangement so that I have some visible evidence of their commitment and so that their involvement in the writing center will appear on their report cards.

2. Explain that, by our next meeting, students *will know how many periods* per week they are willing to staff the center, and *which periods* those will be. I am very firm about the need for certainty.

They *must arrange all other aspects of their lives* so that the schedule, once distributed, will not have to be changed repeatedly. It never matters how firm I am, however, and each September I have to distribute two to three revisions from October until the new tutors join. Inevitably, tutors belatedly decide to join a capella choir or find they need to add a class or whatever. But at least they don't make such changes lightly, and they quiver a bit before informing me they are not available to tutor when they swore they would be.

At our second evening meeting toward the end of September, I distribute to the tutors a blank copy of our school's weekly nine-period-per-day schedule. Classes meet for eight forty-five-minute periods; after school is a shorter activity period of about thirty-five minutes. Each tutor tells the group when he or she will be available, and we fill out the weekly schedule, smoothing out conflicts as we talk. I have found that students are most agreeable and readily willing to accommodate each other's problems. For example, if both Claire and Beth can tutor only during period six on the same day, then one volunteers to come during period nine instead or decides that she can switch the time she meets with a teacher for another independent study.

The first year, each tutor volunteered to staff the center three times per week during free periods. The second year, the number of periods per week per tutor was reduced to two, so we still covered 18 out of 45 possible class periods, or a total of 40 percent.

Once the schedule is established (or so it seems) all tutors and interested teachers, guidance counselors, and administrators receive a copy with the names of the tutors written in the block of time or period for which they have volunteered. Around the school, however, we post schedules with an "X" marked in each period covered by a tutor, so that prospective clients will not be influenced by tutor personalities and other personal considerations or prejudices. Any client with a real concern may always see me or another teacher to find out who is tutoring during any given period. (We have learned, for example, that some eighth-grade and freshman girls are extremely nervous about being tutored by senior boys; while we recognize and try to capitalize on the social interactions that occur in the writing center, some are just too anxiety producing and, therefore, counterproductive.)

New Tutors

Sometime between December 1 and January 1, the new tutors join the original tutors, so I must prepare a different schedule. So far this has not been too difficult; I show the new tutors the existing schedule and they try to fill in during unassigned periods. If a conflict arises, the tutors who are involved usually work it out together. These students must tutor at least once a week as part of the requirements for the Writing and Responding class, though sometimes a new tutor volunteers for another period as well. In that case, I try to arrange independent study credit. By January, tutors cover about 28 out of 45 periods, or 62 percent.

Once they begin tutoring, I urge the new tutors to attend our bimonthly evening meetings in order to achieve some group cohesiveness and sense of camaraderie, but I do not require attendance. All the tutors meet informally at our Christmas party and end of-the-year barbecue where the only "task" is poster making, usually a riotous and very creative affair. (Our school walls are usually decorated with tutor-made writing center posters characterized by varying degrees of inventiveness or absurdity.)

Student Writers

Highland Park High School students may use the writing center in two ways: they may drop in or make an appointment in advance. If students wish to make an appointment, they go to the writing center in the library where they find one of the "X" marked schedules posted on the bulletin board. They sign their names over the "X" in the space for the periods during which they wish to see a tutor. When arriving at the writing center, the tutor looks to see if anyone has signed up for that period. If indeed someone has an appointment, the tutor waits for that student for the first five to eight minutes of that period, explaining to any drop-in clients that someone else is expected but that there may be free time after the middle of the period or even in a few minutes if the appointment isn't kept. Otherwise, students do not need appointments, but may drop in for tutoring any time a tutor is available.

Usually this system works pretty smoothly (except for some specific problems that I will discuss later) unless we are inundated with whole classes assigned by a teacher to visit the writing center. These students must sign up in advance, or the tutors will always be busy with another client when they drop in. Even with appointments, we have difficulty accommodating everyone because no more than one tutor is available per period (though frequently a tutor who happens to be in the library will offer to help an overburdened fellow tutor). However, teachers cooperate by extending deadlines so that all their students have the opportunity to visit the writing center. This is not a typical situation; most of the year we suffer from the opposite problem—*not enough clients*—so we definitely encourage teachers to require visits to the writing center as part of an assignment. We then plaster the school halls with more posters urging writers to make appointments well in advance of the date their assignments are due.

Scheduling Problems

It would be wonderful if the establishment of the "final" schedule signaled the end of administrative problems. In fact, we have encountered several problems that continue to plague us in varying degrees and for which we have devised various solutions.

One problem involves food. Our librarians categorically refuse to allow any food in the library because of mice, smells, rubbish, and so on. So what do we do when some tutors' only free periods are also their only lunch periods? Well, tutors usually run to the cafeteria and gobble a hamburger and then run to the library to tutor. Too often, however, a client who finds the writing center empty upon arrival will scurry away in relief. A better solution has been for tutors to get the vice-principal's permission to eat lunch in a regular class on the days when they must tutor. This arrangement is not possible, however, for the student writers who want to visit the writing center during their lunch periods. Another complication was the rule that students would not be admitted into the library after the first ten minutes of a period. After a powwow including our librarian, building principal, and myself at the beginning of the last school year, that rule was changed to the first twenty minutes of a period, thereby allowing students a bit more time to eat lunch first. This change has helped, but it still severely limits the time for a tutoring session and really does not encourage visits. Aside from scheduling issues, I believe that allowing students to eat in the writing center would also establish a friendlier, more comfortable environment, so I continue to lobby fruitlessly (pun intended).

Another problem is that once in a while the tutor is not in the writing center when he or she has promised to be there. This rarely occurs with new tutors fresh out of Writing and Responding class, who are incredibly optimistic and enthusiastic; rather, it occurs when experienced tutors have spent a few boring periods reading newspapers or doodling in their notebooks waiting in vain for a client. I have tried to convince them of the inevitable *axiom of the high school writing center: if a tutor is not in the writing center, a client will most assuredly appear.* Though I don't like reacting so strongly with students who have volunteered to tutor during their free time (especially when they sit so often without a client), I have arranged with the vice-principal to send a "cut slip" if I discover a tutor's absence. Some absences are unavoidable: if, for example, a tutor attends a field trip or must see a teacher or guidance counselor in an emergency, I request that the tutor post a sign announcing the absence on the writing center bulletin board or inform one of the librarians. Otherwise, if tutors are not legally absent from school, they are charged with a "cut" and must see the vice-principal. After three cuts, the student can no longer tutor. I have stressed the importance of faithful attendance, and tutors understand what happens if a frustrated student finds the writing center empty when the schedule indicates a tutor's presence. Bad publicity travels very quickly, to faculty as well as to other students.

This situation leads to another difficulty that I've hinted at already: our interactions with the librarians, for they are the most visible faculty and inevitably the most involved. Though I check the writing center during most of my free periods (and pull tutors away from their pizzas and french fries in the cafeteria), the librarians answer most of the student questions about the writing center and know better than anyone else if a client is searching for an absent tutor. Therefore, maintaining friendly relations is crucial—but difficult—when the librarians see the writing center encroaching on their territory or creating new problems and more work. What do I do, for example, when the librarians insist that the tutors are just socializing and not working? When they complain that the sessions are too noisy or that a tutor has been rude or uncooperative? Though I might handle a situation very differently, understanding the tutor's tendency to bristle at so many arbitrary rules, I still must sympathize with the librarians' difficulties and support their positions. It seems that my most effective response when confronted with an angry librarian is to listen very carefully and promise to discuss the problem with the tutor, without attacking the librarian or defending the tutor. Only when I believe an issue is of major importance to the functioning of the writing center do I protest enough to cause a conflict. For example, when the librarians were opening the library at 7:30 a.m. and closing it at 2:30 p.m., before ninth period, I convinced our principal to insist that the library be available to students after school. I think that, over the past two years, the librarians have become more comfortable with the writing center, as their roles have become more clearly defined. I also try to encourage the tutors to understand the librarians' importance, and to cooperate by being patient and polite, by returning dictionaries and magazines, by keeping their voices down and not socializing, and, most of all, by not eating.

At first glance, our biggest problem doesn't seem to relate to scheduling: it is involving teachers successfully on a continuing basis. We do have a strong core of support: one special education teacher regularly attends writing center meetings and helps with administrative problems and tutor training, as well as with special activities; my department chairperson is always an important mentor and vocal advocate of the writing center; and at least two other English teachers periodically require that their student writers receive a response from a writing center tutor. Most teachers, however, remain generally indifferent, skeptical, and even, at times, hostile. This situation significantly affects our daily functioning: if teachers would more actively and continually encourage their students to visit the writing center so that we didn't have alternating floods and droughts, morale would improve and tutors would use their tutoring skills more regularly and subsequently strengthen them. As a consequence, tutors would take their commitment to the writing center more seriously and many of our scheduling difficulties would disappear.

I frequently listen with great pleasure to enthusiastic tutors describing successful tutoring sessions; I see tutors meeting with student writers when they are not scheduled to be tutoring. I know they even tutor in the evenings on the phone. That's why I continue to talk at faculty meetings, to meet with teachers during free periods, to stuff fliers and letters in teachers' mailboxes, to print items about the writing center in district newsletters, and to make sure that teachers are notified when their students visit the writing center. I hope that scheduling arrangements can become more productive in exploiting the possibilities for collaborative learning.

7 Developing a Writing Center: What Can a Consultant Do?

Lil Brannon
State University of New York–Albany

When teachers ask me how they might develop a writing center in their school, I usually respond with the question, "What do you mean by a writing center?" If by writing center they mean a "clinic," where poor writers are sent by their teachers to do additional workbook exercises on spelling and subject-verb agreement, then I respond that they don't need an outside consultant to do that. Such "fix-it" laboratories fit right into existing traditional writing curricula, where writing abilities are supposed to develop sequentially, from the learning of punctuation, "proper" usage, and spelling, to the constructing of sentences, then paragraphs, and finally essays. With this model of writing instruction, it's very easy for a writing laboratory to be set up because a curriculum can be easily segmented, with classroom teachers remaining in charge of paragraph development and essay organization and the lab taking charge of sentence level concerns. And this model of a writing lab doesn't take much work either: there are plenty of workbook materials that can be bought for students to fill out; no one needs any special expertise to help the students; and it doesn't take much teacher effort to maintain this laboratory situation. Teachers can just send the "remedial" students down the hall to work on their comma problems.

If, however, those teachers view writing as a central activity of any educational setting and see a writing center as the core of the curriculum, then I would respond that a consultant may be needed in order to get things started. Such an idea of a writing center challenges the conventional wisdom of most faculty, offering in place of the segmented curriculum a holistic view of writing. The writing center becomes a place where writers come (they aren't sent by teachers) to talk about their writing with readers who have not assigned the work and who will not evaluate it. It is a place where writers can find an informal context for talking and raising questions about a particular

55

assignment or a draft in progress, not just engage in repetitive exercises;
a place where their ideas matter first and foremost, not where they
mindlessly fill in the blanks or where they only go over the mistakes
in "grammar" that some teacher has already marked. In this writing
center, student writers find readers who will respond to the meaning
the writers are attempting to convey. The goal of a writing conference
is not simply to clean up a piece of writing but to develop writers by
pushing them toward developing greater intellectual complexity in
their work. This writing center is central to the school setting because

writing is the central activity of learning, not a subordinate one where
the writing is used to display what students have already learned.
Redirecting faculty attitudes about writing centers from the more com-
monplace view of them as a remedial "fix-it" clinic means that teachers
must reeducate their colleagues and administrators, showing them that
a richer and more productive notion of a writing center exists.

Yet accomplishing this goal is no easy matter, for redirecting faculty's
and administrators' attitudes means making institutional change. This
change involves a change of attitude that entails turning teachers and
administrators into writers themselves so that they experience once
again the power of shaping their experiences through writing. A
writing center can become the natural outgrowth of such experience,
for writers know that what matters most to them is their ideas, that
writers need readers, that writers need to talk about their work to
people who are not there to judge them but to respond to what they
are saying. Establishing a successful writing center demands, then,
that teachers understand as much as the students about the complex
processes involved in composing. Teachers will come to use and value
a writing center, I believe, if they have had immersion in the concepts
of learning to write, have reflected on that learning, and have had
some time to plan and raise questions about how their teaching can
enable students to become better writers. Institutional change means,
then, changing teachers' minds: those who have used traditional
methods in their teaching of writing must come to understand that
the motive to learn how to write comes from having something to say
to people who matter to the writer.

But where does one begin, faced with an entire school faculty, some
of whom have never heard of the writing process, much less a writing
center? Most writing centers have begun as the vision of one person
who has gained some knowledge of the field of composition and who
senses what an opportunity such a center can be for students. Yet,
though one person must have the vision and the energy to see it
through, that person will not be able to get it off the ground if trust

has not been built first among fellow teachers, so that the project doesn't seem suspicious—a way to build a power base for oneself or a means of getting out of doing some other work. It is important, too, to build trust with the administration, for they are the ones who ultimately must provide space, time, and materials for the center. Without their support there will be no center. When writing centers have failed to develop, it has been because this groundwork was not laid properly. That groundwork begins, one should remember, during those short conversations in the lunch room about teaching writing, those times when one was successful at helping students with their work, the many hours spent developing curriculum or in being a supportive colleague and an eager contributor. Those colleagues who have always worked productively and cooperatively in the past are certainly the ones to introduce first to the idea of a writing center. Perhaps, a small group of teachers could visit a writing center in the area, preferably a high school center, but if one is not nearby, a college center would do. One's own enthusiasm for the project, in my experience, becomes contagious. Once there is some general support, then it is time to think about the advantages of having an outside consultant.

Often once the groundwork is laid for a writing center, those on the supportive team have gained enough knowledge, motivation, and expertise to develop and sustain the center on their own. Yet these qualities are often not enough when facing the political realities in schools. One such reality is that academics tend to look to "experts" for advice. Equally true is that they seldom see their fellow colleagues as those experts. An outside consultant can supply the same knowledge, experience, and drive as those who have laid the groundwork for the writing center, and they can provide the often needed "expertise" that only an outsider can bring. The way that faculty interact with one another also creates another political problem. Faculty look to their colleagues for support; they view each other as equals. A faculty reeducation program such as one demanded by the development of a writing center changes that normal dynamic if a fellow teacher is in charge. It would be difficult, I am sure, for a colleague to raise a question about another colleague's teaching or to challenge an administrator. An advantage of having an outside consultant is that the consultant can point out problems and offer constructive criticism without being seen as destructive or as being a self-promotor. Finally, an outside consultant can assist in designing inservice workshops and faculty development programs to work within the political realities of schools. In a project I was involved in on Long Island, for example, the teachers knew that, if the high school English department was not squarely behind the center, the center would fail because the rest of the faculty looked to the department for direction in how they should use writing in their classrooms. Not all the twenty-five English teachers, however, knew about innovations in the teaching of writing over the last two decades, so an inservice course that would train all the English department faculty on methods of teaching writing and would build a writing center as the core of such a program seemed entirely appropriate. Yet in another high school where I was a consultant in New Jersey, the faculty faced a different problem: their center needed the support of faculty across the curriculum, particularly the science and social studies teachers. Because the district was small, faculty had little time during or after school to devote to developing a writing center and at that time they had no language arts supervisor who might serve as a central leader, devoting some of his or her time to the project. A writing-across-the-curriculum-project seemed like a reasonable starting point, and a writing center as an outgrowth of that experience, a likely outcome.

Selecting a consultant, though, takes time, for it is crucial to find the right person with whom to work. I think faculty should talk to a variety of consultants before choosing the one that seems best for the school. In order to develop that initial list of consultants to interview, teachers need to talk to other districts and ask who has worked with them on their writing program. One should not rule out as a consultant those whose published work teachers enjoy; often if they cannot work with a school because of travel distance or prior commitments, they can recommend knowledgeable and flexible people in the area. As teachers interview possible consultants, they should beware of the prepackaged programs or all-purpose inservice models. For a writing center to be an outgrowth of an inservice educational experience, that inservice program needs to be tailor-made to fit the needs, relationships, and commitments of a particular school. I think that working with one consultant or a consultant team is the best: they design the program with the faculty, attend every inservice session, observe the classroom, set up the center. There is continuity and a consistent point of view represented. I have, however, seen schools work with multiple consultants, each one bringing particular expertise to bear on the training of faculty and the development of the center. This model works best if the person or faculty team in charge of designing the center has the ability to provide the necessary continuity—that is, is able to build bridges for the faculty from one consultant's workshop to another's and to provide consistency in the development of the center.

Inservice programs, in general, and those focusing on writing centers, in particular, need to be designed to accommodate the special needs and requirements of each individual school. Yet there are some principles I would suggest groups follow if they decide to work with an outside consultant. First, *when* to have an inservice program is almost as crucial a decision as whether or not to have one at all. Inservice programs, I believe, whenever possible should be designed to take place during the school day or, where districts have them, on days set aside for teacher education. Workshops after school or on Saturdays, while they do attract the most dedicated of teachers, nonetheless, "capture" them either when they are the most tired (after school) or when they should be at home with their families. I have found when schools or districts are supportive of such programs, they will find substitutes for teachers so that they can attend workshops. As a consultant, I have had to be flexible in designing workshops: working with half of the teachers for the first half of the day and the second half the other half of the day so that fewer substitutes needed to be hired. And I have brought with me graduate students from my university, many of whom are high school teachers on leave or former high school teachers, to serve as substitutes and teaching models for faculty. I have also offered summer institutes for faculty on the teaching of writing where writing centers were the focal point and natural outgrowth of the workshops. Where the summer programs have been the most successful has been in those schools that provided some follow-up for those teachers during the school year. Follow-up should include both workshops for the entire group and individual conferences for teachers and writing center staff.

Second, a workshop format is, I think, the best model for learning. Besides experiencing materials and trying out the new methods for teaching writing, teachers need to write themselves, share their writing with colleagues, and hear responses to their work. Faculty can profit from trying out various ways of responding to each other's work and revising their initial drafts to meet expectations of their readers. Engaging in such activity demonstrates how writers need readers and how writers can profit from hearing readers' questions. All the mystery of what might happen in a writing center diminishes when teachers' attitudes about the nature of writing begin to change. Those nagging questions about writing centers come from the traditional view of writing: Will someone do the work for the students? Will all mistakes be corrected? Can students help other students or will it be like the blind leading the blind? In these situations the teacher is the authority over all knowledge about writing and students are the receivers of that knowledge. The writing center model supplants those traditional notions by giving the writer the authority to make choices about the writing and by placing the reader, whether it be teacher or fellow student, in the position of raising questions about those choices.

Third, time needs to be set aside for informal talks during the school day, both for the consultant to talk to the teachers and for the teachers to talk with each other. This time might be used for the consultant to teach a model lesson or a series of lessons while other teachers observe and then later discuss what happened. The consultant, too, could visit classes of teachers and discuss what was happening during that class. Since a consultant is not a supervisor who must play an evaluative role, teachers often appreciate the visit and are often more willing to discuss the things that are failing to happen in the classroom. But most important is time for the consultant to meet with each teacher alone to talk about teaching and writing, to hear how the writing center is working for the students, to listen to what is going on and what needs to happen next. Teachers also need time during the school day, about once per week, to talk to one another about the project. This can be done by assigning teachers with the same duty period or preparation period to small task groups. In these groups teachers share what is going on in their classrooms, read articles in common, raise questions that need to be addressed, plan classroom research projects, develop new ways of working with the writing center, and plan ways of introducing more faculty to the writing center.

A writing center can be a place where writers explore ideas and engage in inquiry about their subjects. Modern views of writing instruction show us, if our practice hasn't done so already, that there is no one-shot inoculation against all writing ills. There isn't even a good way to separate out various components of writing. Learning to write happens while writing. One learns to spell, learns the language of texts, learns to construct ideas and shape them by writing and reading the writing of others. And that learning becomes directed and purposeful when the writer's needs and questions become the framework for instruction rather than a prescribed workbook or a teacher-initiated syllabus. If we persist with the traditional view of the writing lab, then those who participate in such a program, both teachers and students, will stay on the fringes of academic life, being labeled as "remedial." And others who could profit from the idea of a writing center will never set foot in the door for fear of being labeled as dumb. A writing center, however, is central to all writers, for every writer profits from having readers, those who can raise questions about a draft in progress or even celebrate a job well done. A writing center, because it demands a change of faculty attitude, finally is more difficult to construct. Yet one knows the effort was all worthwhile when students and faculty enter into dialogue, talking to each other about their writing. Every school should see itself as a community of writers. Every school should have a writing center.

II Functioning

8 Training Peer Tutors for the Secondary School Writing Center

Elizabeth Ackley
Indian Hill High School
Cincinnati, Ohio

Writing center tutors must first be writers themselves, not necessarily the E. B. Whites of tomorrow, but students who share a concern for writing as the process of thinking. In addition, they must be listeners who care about the tutees and their writing problems. The tutors must be immersed in the writing process as theory and practicum; they should know strategies to help at every stage of the writing process; and they should continue to write while they tutor.

After establishing the preceding criteria for tutors and selecting forty students from the junior and senior classes, the appropriate administrators of Indian Hill School District and I decided that the training would have to occur before school started. I divided the students into two groups to attend what they have dubbed "English Camp." For twenty hours (four hours per day for five days) the students come to English Camp to train for tutoring. Once school starts, they are assigned for one period per one semester to the writing center, which is open for all students every period of every day and after school on Tuesdays and Thursdays. The tutors continue to keep journals and they fill out record sheets that are filed in the tutee's writing center folder. The record sheets contain space to record information such as a statement of the problems, a description of the tutoring, and comments by the tutor. For this work, the tutors receive one-half credit and a guaranteed "A" in the course called "Advanced Methods of Composition." The guaranteed grade is based on the assumption that, for the program to succeed, the tutors must maintain a standard of excellence or be withdrawn from the program. So far, that situation has not arisen. The number of students selected, based on a seven-period day, allows two to three tutors per period both first and second semesters. Luckily, the study halls scheduled by the computer have been evenly distributed over the course of the day and the semesters, and scheduling has been no problem.

Since writing as process is the philosophical basis for the program, each summer day begins with the students writing for fifty minutes. At the end of the fifty minutes, we convene and converse for ten. During the second hour each day, the training continues with discussion of the required reading. Before the summer session begins, the students read Gary Provost's *Make Every Word Count* (1983). This book's primary point is that everyone can be a writer and offers "hands on" strategies for getting ideas, writing drafts, and improving expression by tightening, sharpening, deleting. Provost contends that every word must "work" for a place in the composition, and he shows students various techniques to "make every word count" (4). Also on the first day, we read and discuss "Teach Writing As Process Not Product," by Donald Murray (Graves 1983, 89–92) and "An Approach to Writing" by Peter Elbow (1981, 6–12). These two short articles emphasize the foundation for seeing writing as a process and as thinking. Both authors emphasize the necessity for being able to remove self from writing and to evaluate the written word. This second hour each day reinforces the concepts upon which the program is based by allowing for discussion of those concepts as recorded by leaders in the writing-as-process movement.

During the third hour of each day, we share what we have written during the first hour, an essential experience for the training, because, in sharing, we learn how to listen and respond to what we hear. Before beginning the process of listening, we discuss the qualities of a good listener and before we begin to respond, we talk about the kinds of comments that are most helpful to the writer. All read their pieces twice. After the first reading, the responses should be positive: "I liked the section describing your little brother's face," or "The description of our second grade teacher made her seem alive again." After the second reading, the tutors may question sections of the piece: "I don't understand how your little brother got the bat out of the tree," or "Do you think more detail about her eyes would let us see her better?" The writer makes notes and later chooses which responses to use in revising the piece. This writing and responding illuminates for the tutors the kinds of responses that mean the most to them as writers and instills in them techniques and attitudes that they need to be tutors once the school year begins. As we read more articles, the questioning and responding reflect the more extensive and diverse strategies that the authors provide (see the reference section at the end of this chapter).

At the end of each day, we spend the hour simulating possible tutoring experiences. On the first day I have tutors from the past year come to the class and re-enact situations that they had. The new tutors can then see the diversity of the students they will tutor, the diversity of the writing problems, and the diversity of the tutors themselves in how they dealt with the problems. We discuss how the tutor could have handled the tutee or the problem differently and what acted positively for the tutee. By holding up actual sessions for reflection, the new tutors readily see that each session will be different, even if some of the strategies for help can work in many situations: they see the human element.

At this point in the required reading, Beverly Clark's *Talking about Writing* (1985) proves invaluable. In chapter seven, "Coach or Director?", she presents several tutoring sessions as scripts; we read them aloud and discuss the merits of each. In chapter eight, "Getting Started," much of what we have already discussed or experienced as writers and listeners comes to focus on us as tutors: how to assess the tutee's attitudes and needs, how to listen to the tutee's problems and paper, how to respond positively to the paper, how to elicit response from the tutee about how to improve the paper. And also at this point in the reading, I introduce firsthand experiences from directors and tutors who have written to *The Writing Lab Newsletter.* My students realize that we have progressed from reading about the theory of writing, the strategies of writing, the role of the tutor, to the actual experiences of the tutor. One article by William O. Shakespeare, a student tutor from Brigham Young University, presents the various kinds of students who come to the center: the apathetic, the rebellious, the copycat, and gives advice on how to deal with them. Elray L. Pedersen, another student tutor, also of Brigham Young, addresses kinds of responses to use. And yet another tutor, Anne Mattison, of the College of St. Benedict, reviews her experience as a tutor by explaining how important thinking is to tutoring and writing. Even though these institutions are colleges, the problems and solutions faced by their tutors and tutees have much in common with those in the secondary schools.

Chapter nine of Beverly Clark's book gets "Down to Business." She presents various techniques: being silent, mirroring, confirming, recording, asking questions, modeling, reading aloud, agreeing on an assignment, deferring to the student, using appropriate body language, marking progress, and ending. Again, this chapter reinforces the ideas and the strategies that we have read and discussed. We further discuss the application of these responses to situations that we role-play. And the students see that, while no one procedure works all the time, the choices they have before them can be molded to just about any situation: if having a difficulty with logic, recording what has been said may make that student aware of a digression; reading a paper aloud may help a student who has many mechanical errors; asking questions may help a student who cannot think of a topic, and so on. The tutors are quick to recognize the value of the diverse approaches we have discussed and enacted.

At this point in the training, we also concentrate on helping each other with specific kinds of problems that usually receive attention during the revision of a paper. We discuss "tightening," "sharpening," and "showing not telling," and actually work with the writing we have done each morning to revise for better sentences and papers. We "tighten" such sentences as "All I wish is that the administration would be more consistent when they deal out punishments that are for different offenses," or "The thing that makes me the maddest is to have something biting me inside my shirt collar." We all rewrite the sentences and then compare and discuss the twenty different versions to decide which one may be most effective.

We also talk about "sharpening" prose and rewrite sentences that use too many "to be" constructions, "it," and "there." Shakespeare, for instance, in *Macbeth*, could have said, "This tyrant whose sole name IS a blister on our tongues, was once thought honest." He chose, instead to say "This tyrant whose sole name BLISTERS our tongues, was once thought honest." The tutors are quick to see the difference. Macrorie, in *Writing To Be Read* (1984), says, however, that "Sharpening writing is not as black and white a matter as this . . . suggests. Many of the changes dictated . . . are debatable, and only a person considering the total context of a word or phrase can see whether or not it should be retained" (67). The discussion leads us to audience, purpose, and context. And the students are learning yet another avenue in writing as process, yet another avenue to pursue in eliciting from themselves and from their tutees more forceful, effective writing by "making every word count." Most tutors at this point see the dovetailing of the writing, the reading, the discussing, the role-playing that we have done.

We spend at least one hour discussing "showing writing," moving from generalities to specifics, because this is a predominent problem for the tutees who come to the center. I have adapted my material from Provost (1983, 34–35). The objectives in the plan are to recognize the differences between "telling" writing and "showing" writing, to reinforce the use of concrete details in place of or in support of generalities, and to apply the differences between "telling" writing and "showing" writing to the revision process. Examples abound, and although the following two passages concern a scene at a bus stop, the passages illustrate the difference:

> Each morning I ride the bus to school. I wait along with the other people who ride my bus. Sometimes the bus is late and we get

angry. Some guys start fights and stuff just to have something to do. I'm always glad when the bus finally comes. (a seventh-grade student)

A bus arrived. It discharged its passengers, closed its doors with a hiss and disappeared over the crest of a hIll. Not one of the people waiting at the bus stop had attempted to board. One woman wore a sweater that was too small, a long skirt, white sweater socks, and house slippers. One man was in his undershirt. Another man wore shoes with the toes cut out. There was something wrong with these people. They made faces. A mouth smiled at nothing and unsmiled, smiled and unsmiled. A head shook in vehement denial. Most of them carried brown paper bags rolled tight against their stomachs. (Doctorow 1971, 15)

We discuss the obvious differences in the two passages, and the students quickly understand the difference in "showing" and "telling." They also quickly note that Doctorow wisely uses "there" and a "to be" construction and the effect that the construction has taken in context. We then propose questions to ask the seventh grader which would lead that student to "showing" writing: Does any one person come to mind when you picture yourself waiting? How is the person dressed? How do you know the others are angry? Exactly how do they look? What do they say? How do you show you are glad when the bus arrives?

We write our own "showing" paragraphs on such topics as "The dog was mean," "The child was incredibly filthy," "The room was a mess," "The pizza was fantastic." We use the reading-responding-reading-responding process for each selection written, and the students become involved in one of the most critical experiences that they will have as tutors: how to "show" not "tell." The paragraphs that they write on the same topic prove the necessity of using details to create intended meaning.

Whenever possible, the tutor takes the tutee through the process of writing a paper from the prewriting stage through the final draft. In suggesting how to structure these ongoing conferences, I give them Garrison's (1981) cardinal rule—"Only one objective is considered during a conference, and conferences are focused in this sequence" (101):

Prewriting:	tutor praises whatever specific details and facts the student already has and elicits more by asking questions or by asking for examples.
Organization:	tutor helps student find answers to these questions—What do these facts say? What do I want to say about these facts? Do these facts add up to anything? How will I organize these facts?

Rough Draft:	tutor reads for organization and focus on controlling idea.
Correctness:	tutor has student read aloud portions with run-on sentences, incorrect usage, etc., so student can hear errors; student is referred to materials covering specific problems in mechanics.
Word Choice/ Spelling:	tutor calls attention to especially vivid, apt diction and helps student to find more colorful expressions; student must correct misspelled words.

Dawe and Dornan (1981) also promote this process of conferencing:

> If first reading reveals that a paper has too little content or insufficient detail, we point out the problem and ask the writer to rewrite. As we work down the list in successive conferences, we find that solving one problem tends to help resolve others. Once a student has added specifics, for instance, organization and coherence tend to improve. (76)

Each afternoon when we role-play, I give the students hypothetical situations and they alternate playing tutee and tutor. The situations that we find most typical involve prewriting, organization, and using specific detail: A freshman has been asked by his teacher to compare two characters from two different short stories. Not having read either story, the tutor asks the freshman to talk about the characters. The tutor asks such questions as "What did you first notice about the character? Why does the author intend you to notice that? What does the detail tell you about the character? And so on. The tutee writes down responses and begins to map-cluster them. The tutor uses the same procedure for the next character; the tutee begins to draw lines from cluster to cluster to show relationships. The tutee goes to another table to write, and returns when something has been put down on paper. The conferencing continues.

A senior comes in with a college application essay topic which asks that the student write about the most meaningful high school experience. The student tells the tutor, "Nothing I've done is more meaningful than anything else." The tutor asks the student to list all activities and classes that come to mind, and then asks if the student can number or list them according to the kinds of experiences that occurred in those instances. As it turns out, the student groups all music experiences near the top because, "By myself I'm not creative, but with the musical groups I feel we create something impressive." Obviously, the student now has an essay topic.

The journals that the students keep during the summer provide them with ideas for assignments all year. But just as important to the training, the tutors must continue to keep the journals during the semester that they are tutoring. What they write keeps them in touch with themselves as writers and as tutors, and what they write can provide two-way communication between the writing center director and each tutor. I collect the twenty journals on Friday, read them during my writing center period, and return them to their mailboxes in the center on Monday. I find this procedure to be an invaluable way of keeping in touch with what is going on in the writing center. I teach five classes per day and am assigned to the writing center for one period (as is every other English teacher in lieu of study hall, cafeteria duty, and so forth).

In making their entries, the students often write about a particular tutoring session in which they felt either success or failure or frustration; I respond as helpfully as I can. They may have particular problems (for example, ESL students, one tutee with special revision blocks, and others) and the journal communication allows me to refer them to specific articles and handbooks in the writing center (see the reference list at the end of this chapter). They may simply free write and ask for my response before they revise. But this continuing involvement further trains them to be even more responsive to their own thinking and writing and, therefore, more responsive to the tutees they will meet. Again, and most important, the journals allow me a vicarious experience in the center, and they allow me to keep in touch with tutors that I no longer have in class.

The tutors' responses to the training and the tutoring give substance to the experience. One of the best tutors wrote in her journal, "I always thought that my math ability indicated a business/computer career. But now that I've learned how much I love crawling around in someone else's head and seeing how people think, I want to teach them how to do it better. I want to teach." Another wrote, "I never realized that being in touch with my own thinking could show me how to help others get in touch with theirs." Still another noted, "I had always been told not to *ever* use any form of the verb 'to be,' 'it,' or 'there.' Talk about writing block! I now know to eliminate with thought and prudence. *There are* no absolutes in writing. *It would be silly if there were.*" I particularly liked the last summer entry of one student: "Thank you to all of us."

References

Clark, Beverly. *Talking about Writing*. Ann Arbor: University of Michigan Press, 1985.

Dawe and Dornan. *One to One: Resources for Conference-Centered Writing*. New York: Little-Brown, 1981.

Doctorow, E. L. *The Book of Daniel.* New York: Random House, 1971.

Elbow, Peter. "An Approach to Writing." In *Writing with Power,* 6–12. New York: Oxford University Press, 1981.

———. *Writing with Power.* New York: Oxford University Press, 1981. See pages 39–46; 78–93; 121–145; 199–215; 216–225.

Garrison, Roger H. *How a Writer Works.* New York: Harper and Row, 1981.

Graves, Richard L., ed. *Rhetoric and Composition.* Upper Montclair, N.J.: Boynton/Cook Publishers, Inc., 1983. See Murray, 263–68; Perl, 304–10; Sommers, 328–37.

Macrorie, Ken. *Writing to Be Read.* Upper Montclair, N.J.: Boynton/Cook Publishers, Inc., 1984.

Murray, Donald. "Teaching Writing as a Process, Not a Product." In *Rhetoric and Composition,* edited by Richard L. Graves, 89–92. Upper Montclair, N.J.: Boynton/Cook Publishers, Inc., 1983.

Olson, Gary A., ed. *Writing Centers: Theory and Administration.* Urbana, Ill.: NCTE, 1984. See Olson, 155–162; Simard, 197–204; Friedlander, 206–14; Fearing and Keats, 215–23.

Provost, Gary. *Make Every Word Count.* Cincinnati: Writer's Digest Books, 1983.

Sudol, Ronald., ed. *Revising: New Essays for Teachers of Writing.* Urbana, Ill.: ERIC/NCTE, 1982. See Fulwiler, 100–108; Ruszkiewicz, 144–48; Spear, 152–62.

9 Training of Professional Staff

Anne Wright
Hazelwood West High School
Hazelwood, Missouri

The Hazelwood School District

In spite of educators' knowledge about planning and preparation, we often seem to start new projects with the old "sink or swim" attitude. After four years of operation, we can safely say that our writing lab at Hazelwood West High School has learned to "swim," although the training of personnel has been haphazard, at best.

Much of the success of the writing labs in the three Hazelwood high schools has been due to careful planning of procedures and objectives before the labs opened in 1983. There was no personnel training in methods of tutoring, but at least all the teachers who were to staff the labs met in a one-week workshop in June to develop plans for the fall. The plans made at the workshop solved many problems that the professional staff would have faced as the labs started operating, and, therefore, allowed the teachers to concentrate on learning how to tutor effectively and how to use a computer for word processing.

At our summer workshop, we decided which students would constitute our clientele, how many students we could tutor in one class period, what the role of the labs would be in the total school writing program, what record keeping procedures we would follow, and what supplies and equipment we would need.

After much discussion, we decided that we would target for our clientele that first year both remedial students and those who needed enrichment. Students in English classes would be our primary targets for the first year, although we decided we would offer the services of the professional staff to teachers in other disciplines who asked for assistance in preparing writing assignments or who wanted a lab staff member to come to their classes and get the students started on writing assignments. We followed these plans rather faithfully during the first

year, but we learned very quickly that it was hard to tell an "enrichment" student from a "developmental" student, and we didn't quibble
over the ability level of any student who was referred to us by an
English teacher.

Another important decision that was made in the summer workshop
determined how students could get access to the labs. Since all our
students must take six classes in a six-hour day, the only system that
seemed feasible was a referral system. English teachers would decide
when students needed some remediation or enrichment, sign them up
to come to the lab, and send a referral form with them to tell the lab
staff what the students were to work on. We also followed this plan
carefully the first year, but we have since discovered that most students
are really self-referrals, asking their English teachers or any other
teacher they think will release them from class for passes to the lab.
Most teachers don't fill out referral forms any more; they rely on the
students to tell us what they need to work on. (As you can imagine,
sometimes a problem develops from this lack of communication with
the teachers, but we have not had any serious repercussions.)

The second topic we discussed in our summer workshop concerned
how many students the labs could effectively tutor in one class period.
Each of the three labs is staffed by one English teacher and one teacher
assistant, every period of the day. If our goal was to give individual
assistance to students referred to us, we knew we had to set some
limits on the number of students signed up for each hour. We finally
decided to design a sign-up sheet that provided places for one week's
daily schedule. The space for each day is divided into six squares, one
for each class period, and each period has space for six students'
names. We would try to help more if they showed up, but we hoped
that, when teachers saw that all six spaces were filled, they would not
send any more students. We also explained to the teachers in department meetings that sometimes two students would be capacity for us,
if they were students with severe problems who really had to have
one-to-one attention. To summarize, we set parameters, but we try to
be as accommodating as possible and still provide quality instruction
to individual students.

Developing a philosophical basis for our goals was probably the
most important accomplishment of the summer workshop. We decided
that we wanted to be more than just a tutoring service; we wanted to
provide leadership for the total writing program of the school. We
wanted to foster a positive attitude toward writing among the students.
Therefore, we agreed to accept and publicize all announcements about
writing contests; to buy and maintain a professional library of resources

about teaching writing; to use computers for word processing; to send letters to the parents of all students who came to the labs for the first time, telling them about the new service the school was offering students; to promote writing across the curriculum; and to participate in professional writing conferences whenever possible.

We have continued to carry out all these functions and have added a few more. At Hazelwood West High School, we now sponsor a writing club, which publishes a literary magazine and conducts an all-school writing contest with cash prizes each year. In all three labs, computers now play a much larger role, since we now have enough for a class of twenty-five to work at the same time. The increase in computer activity has made us much more conscious of the importance of having a philosophical basis because it would be very easy to become simply a computer lab. With our goals clearly in mind, we try very hard to maintain tutoring as our reason for being and improving writing as our major goal. We still insist that it is essential to have as a staff member an English teacher who knows writing theory and not capitulate to a few administrators' suggestions that a teacher-clerk who knows how to use computers could run the labs.

Next, we turned our attention to record keeping and what procedures we would follow to obtain the information we would need for records. Those procedures are explained in detail in chapter 14 of this book, but to summarize briefly, we decided that extensive record keeping would be beneficial for two reasons. First, a new program nearly always has to be justified after its initial year. We needed records to justify our existence. Second, we needed records to help us evaluate our program. From our records we can see how many students we are serving in each of the ability categories (remedial, developmental, and enrichment). We can see how many students are entering writing contests, which teachers are referring students, what classes most of the students come from, and what departments make use of the lab. From this information, we can make adjustments in our program.

Finally, in that summer planning session, we made decisions about what supplies and equipment we would need. In addition to the computer, disk drives, and printer, and the supplies necessary to run them (paper and disks, software), we needed books for students' reference and books on writing theory and practice for teachers. We also asked the district printing shop to print some posters on the offset press for us to use in the high schools to promote the writing labs. The printing shop also printed on NCR paper the forms for the records we wanted to keep carbons of. We listed as necessary equipment a filing cabinet, desks for the staff, a bookcase, and chairs and tables for students. When school started in the fall, all of these supplies and equipment were ready for us.

Other School Districts

Several school districts in the metropolitan St. Louis area, of which Hazelwood is a part, now have some form of writing lab. When Hazelwood opened its three labs in 1983, only one other one existed in the county, and it was started the same year. As codirector of the Gateway Writing Project (part of the National Writing Project), I have been in touch with staff in most of the new labs. What I have seen in the way of professional staff development has been similar to the Hazelwood experience, except that most of the other schools don't seem to have the paid week of summer planning. What is happening is that most of the teachers chosen to staff the labs have extensive training and experience in teaching writing. Many have been through the Gateway Writing Project summer institute. In the Parkway School District, for example, writing labs have been or are in the process of being established in at least two high schools. The teacher chosen to direct the one at Parkway South High School attended the institute last summer, visited the lab at my school, and consulted with me extensively before school started in 1986. Teachers from Parkway West have also been to visit our lab, and one of them attended the summer institute in 1985. The department chair and the first director of the Pattonville High School writing center were both Gateway-trained people. At Langston Middle School, in the city of St. Louis, the staff members who direct the two writing labs are both Gateway alumnae.

So what I am seeing in this area is not training on how to run writing labs, but training in the form of writing theory and practice. I believe that is exactly how it should be. The staff of each individual lab must work out procedures that will suit the particular needs and restrictions of their school. While planning time similar to what we had in Hazelwood is desirable, what is most essential is simply to choose staff members who have studied recent research and theory and know how to adapt what they have learned to the teaching of writing. They will learn quickly what they need to know about running a lab.

10 Filling the Room: Public Relations

James Upton
Burlington Community High School
Burlington, Iowa

Attracting, cajoling, or enticing students (and staff) to utilize a writing center obviously depends upon the nature of the services offered in the center. Our center, "The Write Place," has three major services: (1) to provide remediation, reinforcement, and enrichment of all communication skills to all students on a request or referral basis; (2) to provide "The Write Place" personnel in all classrooms so that they may introduce and give practice in traditional writing skills (for example, essay exams, research papers, study skills, and so forth) and also introduce and assist with writing-as-learning activities; (3) to provide a center for staff exploration, development, and sharing of writing-as-learning activities. The following discussion is based on our experiences. Please feel free to utilize or modify any of these ideas for your center.

Essential to "filling the room" is raising student, staff, and community consciousness about the center—and this must begin even before the center opens. Such consciousness-raising activities must then continue once the center begins operation. We began research into a writing center and began writing formal proposals to establish one almost three years before the center formally opened. We also spent much of this time discussing and debating the need for and design of such a center within the language arts department and with all other departments and staff members. We tried to make all staff members aware of the potential uses and benefits of such a center and tried to establish the broadest possible base of support. During this time, we were also discussing the proposed center with any and all service and civic clubs, school related organizations, and any other interested groups. We began to offer many of the center's services on an informal basis and used this work to help refine our design for the center and to help raise consciousness. Although we have no way to judge the effect of this "informal promotion," we believe our efforts were worthwhile.

Before the formal opening of the center, we held a full faculty meeting to explain the nature, operation, and services of "The Write Place" for both faculty and students. We encouraged all faculty members to recommend that their students use the facilities and services of the center. Just as important, we urged the faculty to refer students out of their classes and to invite center personnel into their classrooms for assistance in traditional writing activity and for writing-as-learning. We gave each staff member a copy of the flier the students would receive and a large supply of "appointment request forms" for assistance in and from "The Write Place."

Before the official opening, we also made signs and posters that simply said "The Write Place." We began daily announcements on the public address system that played upon the "write" and "right" idea. As the official opening drew nearer, we wrote articles about the center for the school newspaper, the monthly building newsletter for parents, the district newsletter for parents, and the local news media. These efforts have been continued and expanded. In the monthly building newsletter, we have invited parents to visit "The Write Place" to pick up writing and study aids for their children. We have also urged them to encourage their children to utilize the services of the center.

We continue to try to heighten consciousness and use of "The Write Place" in several ways. A minor but important point was to have our letterhead stationery and memo pads printed. We hope to sponsor a contest later this year to encourage students to create a logo for the center because we think this separate identity is important.

In addition to the services that we offer, the center also publishes three types of publications. "The Write Place" reproduces articles about writing, learning, and writing as-learning for the staff, and we always encourage staff to use all of the services of the center for themselves and their students. "The Write Stuff" is a newsletter written by and for the faculty and contains editorials, reviews of professional materials, sharings of successful classroom techniques, and creative works. Each issue also contains encouragement for use of "The Write Place." We also publish "Student Stuff," a newsletter of student fiction and non-fiction (in which we urge all students to utilize the center). We print all contributions to "Student Stuff." The submission basket is located in "The Write Place."

We have devised a number of interesting ways to get students to visit "The Write Place." In addition to having the submission basket for "Student Stuff," we have also made a "Contest Corner" in the center. We list all of the current writing contests and scholarship competitions, and we sponsor group sharing sessions for all students interested in entering the same contests. We have campaigns to encourage college-bound students to utilize the center's personnel in assisting with college and scholarship essays. We also use the center for small group meetings with visiting speakers and artists.

When the center officially opened, we asked every English instructor to distribute fliers about "The Write Place" and give each student an appointment request form. We asked that the instructors explain the operation of the center and encourage all students to use the center for all communication needs and assistance.

We have begun to utilize student tutors in "The Write Place." We now have the instructors and student tutors visit each class early in the semester to introduce themselves, explain the operation of the center, and encourage students to use the services that are available. We ask student tutors to do most of the talking and most of the "promoting."

We have expanded the use of center personnel and student tutors in an important way. If there are no center requests, we send at least some of our personnel into writing classrooms to help confer with and tutor students or groups of students in the classroom. We will expand this in-class conferencing and tutoring into several content area classrooms later this year because we believe this is very important. We always have our tutors leave the students with a strong suggestion/invitation to make an appointment with "The Write Place" for follow-up help.

Some instructors give students "extra credit" for verified visits to the center. The building now handles all of our scheduling and report cards, and we are able to send notes on report cards urging students to visit "The Write Place." We are also trying to do a more effective job of coordinating major research projects among content area teachers and language arts teachers and "The Write Place," to involve more effectively the center personnel in aiding students who have such major projects.

Another of our promotion devices was to place a "coupon" in the school newspaper to help stimulate awareness and use of the center. The coupon entitled the bearer to "One Free Visitation in The Write Place," and while most students know that there is no charge for center services, we did have students who utilized the coupon.

On the professional level, we sponsor informal coffee sharings for all faculty to discuss writing and writing-as-learning ideas. Through these meetings we urge faculty to use and we encourage students to use the services of "The Write Place."

There are times that the center has more requests for services than we can handle, but this is an enjoyable problem. There are times when no one is utilizing any of the services or personnel of the center, and this is most frustrating. We have accepted the fact that simply making the services available to students and staff is not enough; we also have to create the need to use the center. We sometimes wonder if our efforts are worth the outcome, but then we ask ourselves, "What did these students who use the center do before it opened? What will they do if we close?" The answer to those questions is as obvious as the reason why we will keep offering and promoting "The Write Place."

11 Types of Student Clients

Ellen H. Brinkley
Western Michigan University

A secondary school writing center is for all the students at the school. We say it, and we believe it. What we mean, of course, is that the help is available for all. But not all students will voluntarily drop in for help, and not all students will need the same kind of help.

Early in the planning stages of the Madeira High School Writing Assistance Program, in Cincinnati, Ohio, we decided that, while the center would be available for all, we would focus in particular on two groups of students—those who especially wanted writing assistance and those who especially needed it. Maxine Hairston had identified two groups who benefit most from individual conferences: "highly motivated individuals who, regardless of the grades he or she is making, truly want to improve" and "borderline C-/D students who are hovering on the edge of disaster" (Hairston 1982, 11).

Is there a time to require *all* students to come for a conference? Yes, at the beginning of the school year, especially if the center is new and students don't know what to expect. And, yes, when students are working on long major projects such as research papers. Individual conferences help in such cases when there are so many tasks involved, so many things that can go wrong, so much that's unique about each individual student's work that can't be addressed in a classroom setting.

Before discussing specific kinds of students served by a center, it is important to point out that, at Madeira, as we trained our teachers to do individual conferencing, we especially emphasized the need to avoid taking possession of the student's writing. We reinforced ourselves with this cautionary note periodically. Our purpose was to train student writers to improve their writing skills rather than to "fix" particular pieces of writing for them. Student comments like the following helped us know we were on the right track: "The teacher was able to bring ideas out of my head without telling me directly what to write my paper on. She was then able to help me put my ideas in order that would best fit the paper. . . . In a final sense, the teacher was able to make me work to get my ideas down on paper." Another student commented that the center is "not an easy way out of your writing assignments." She continued, "The teachers just don't blurt out the answers to your questions, but they help you to form your own ideas. This makes you think."

At Madeira we made a special effort to entice our very best students into the lab, partly because they would benefit from our help and partly because we wanted our student body to notice that even the best students come to the center. Because the tutors at Madeira are teachers rather than peers, we could offer constructive help even to senior advanced placement students, who often came in to talk about essays they were writing for college scholarship applications. These students, who usually had a long string of talents and accomplishments to describe, sometimes weren't sure just how to start or shape these essays that had such important, potential consequences. One fellow teacher noted that even valedictorians have come for writing assistance as they prepared those end-of-the-year speeches they wanted so desperately to get just right.

We also saw our most creative students, especially those who wrote poetry. They wanted to share their work and to find more than the praise or puzzled looks they received from classmates' responses. As we sought real audiences for our students' writing, we encouraged them to enter poetry contests, which also generated considerable interest and enthusiasm in individual conferences.

Our best students, then, recognized a good thing when they saw it: they knew the writing center represented a resource that could be used when needed, so they didn't hesitate to seek our help. It is interesting to observe that often our best students came to the center, not to work on regular classroom assignments, but rather when faced with *real* writing situations that mattered to them.

At the other end of the spectrum, we also saw the "basic" students, those who had to "qualify" for their basic-level classes. They came often to our writing center, though sometimes reluctantly at first. They had to be shown that the center was a nonthreatening source of help, something we tried to accomplish by role-playing conference situations in class. When asked about her experience in the center, one such student said, "You go in there feeling really stupid because you feel incompetent. But it is not like that at all; it's very relaxed . . . don't feel stupid because if you go, you are the smart one."

These students, extremely low in self-esteem and devoid of confidence in their writing, benefited immensely from the one-to-one instruction at the center. They came with a variety of problems. For example, they often needed more explanation and help getting started on a writing assignment. They also needed help on specific sentence structure problems. Working individually, we were able to discuss the problems, using the students' own writing. Such sessions, we felt, had significance far outweighing class periods where the whole group might correct sentences produced by a teacher or a textbook.

Another consideration, one we didn't foresee, was that these basic-level students needed the special attention they got in the center. We treated them and their writing with respect. And, yes, sometimes these students talked about more than their writing. Occasionally we heard about problems with boyfriends or parents. At such times we reminded ourselves that establishing rapport is at the heart of the conference method. We remembered Lucy Calkins's caution that "our first job . . . is to be a person, not just a teacher. It is to enjoy, to care, and to respond. We cry, laugh, nod, and sigh. We let the writer know she has been heard" (Calkins 1986, 118–19). In describing his experience with our center, one student said, "I think that when you go in for writing assistance you learn more about the teacher and the teacher also learns more about the student. This is really important."

Other students who really needed our help were the middle-of-the-road students, called "college prep" at Madeira. There weren't as many basic sentence errors to be worked on with this group, but we did a lot of work with helping them to focus their ideas. Sometimes they came in with what they called a "draft" of a paper, but which we noticed was really freewriting, that is, a first effort. So we helped them focus by asking what their most interesting or important ideas were, sometimes turning their papers over as we asked those questions, in order to force them to step back from the details they'd written and sort out their thoughts. One student expressed her experience well: "Writing assistance basically acted as a mirror for my own thoughts. I couldn't focus on anything myself, and there were so many possibilities, I couldn't tell what I wanted to write about. But the teacher pokes and prods and asks the right questions so that I can focus on what I wish to write." Another student said, after reading aloud a paper in conference, "It let me hear what needs to be changed and stirred up some more ideas."

There were other groups of students who especially benefited from working in the center. Shy students who normally never voluntarily spoke out in class sometimes found new confidence as they experienced the encouragement offered by the writing center teacher. On the other hand, the class clowns also benefited, for they were freed from their buddies' expectations to perform and could concentrate on the writing tasks at hand. We realized, too, that one of the benefits of working almost exclusively with the students' writing rather than with textbook materials was that we could easily focus on individual ethnic or cultural language needs as they arose.

We were also pleased when teachers in other content areas stopped in with questions about their own or their students' writing. On rare occasions the principal even wandered in to talk over the wording of a passage written for an important letter or report. Also, if my memory serves me correctly, we answered a grammatical question or two for the superintendent as well. We realized we had become a resource that was truly meant to serve the school community as a whole.

The high school writing center, then, is for all, but especially for those who want it and for those who need it. We who staff such centers are wise to check records periodically to monitor which students are and are not using the center. We then can seek ways to encourage particular types of students so that they all will eventually recognize the benefits of working one-to-one. As one of our students explained, "In a classroom, the teacher is busy helping others, but in Writing Assistance it's your time."

References

Calkins, L. *The Art of Teaching Writing.* Portsmouth, N.H.: Heinemann Educational Books, 1986.

Hairston, M. *A Contemporary Rhetoric.* 3rd ed. Instructor's Manual. Boston: Houghton Mifflin, 1982.

12 Working with Students

Sharon Sorenson

Every student in the school eventually lands in the writing lab, the mainstreamed special education student as well as the academic honors student and everyone in between. It's departmental policy. With a school population of about 1,500 students, one full-time lab instructor, and an operating schedule of five periods per day, the lab may be working with virtually every kind of student on any given day, sometimes within the same period. So how does the lab instructor cope with the variety? In other words, how can the lab instructor offer individualized instruction to the entire spectrum of students and still maintain sanity?

The situation addressed here did not rely on the use of peer tutors. There were dozens of reasons, all the usual ones, but the end result was the same: the lab functioned under the guidance of one instructor. In order to do what the lab was designed to do, that is, offer individualized instruction in all areas of writing, whether for remediation, reinforcement, or enrichment, the approach demanded structure and organization.

First, structure. The facility limited visits to sixteen students at any given time. The sixteen came from one class or a combination of classes; teachers made appointments for their students as space was available. As a result, even though the classes were grouped homogeneously, the lab often received difficult-to-work-with combinations. So, again, structure. Teachers submitted a diagnostic sheet (these are sometimes completed by the students themselves), for each student visiting the lab. The diagnostic sheet, a list of fifty-four possible areas of need, allowed the teacher to merely check a specific item or, if the teacher preferred, to write a detailed note in the space provided. Thus, by checking the student's past record, including test scores and a narrative of previous lab visits, the lab instructor knew what to expect both in terms of ability and in terms of need.

Next, then, the organization. Understanding the students' needs enabled the lab instructor to make logical "assignments" for the lab period. Assignments were made, materials readied, and all information placed at individual study carrels prior to the arrival of each group of students. Then, when students arrived, they found their own diagnostic sheets and seated themselves at their respective study carrels, ready to work.

The structure and organization prior to their visits enabled me to work simultaneously with all kinds of students. The final key that enabled both the lab and the lab instructor to survive, however, was the abundance of materials available. While we used a number of commercially prepared audio-tutorial programs, we also developed our own—two lessons on different levels for each of the fifty-four items on the diagnostic sheet. That was no small task, and we spent a year doing it. The results, however, were worth the effort. Each lesson included an instruction sheet that explained the rules or principles involved in the subject under study. Following the instruction sheet were two exercises, one at an easy-to-moderate level and one at an advanced level (not just more of the same, but requiring a more complicated thought process and a more sophisticated application of the lesson). Accompanying these printed materials was an audiocassette tape. Because all tapes were recorded extemporaneously, the lab instructor, for all practical purposes, was able to talk to the students via tape in the same manner as if talking to each individually. And, as a result, the tape didn't sound like someone reading a script. It wasn't. Instead, students heard comments like these: "Now, if you missed that one, you don't understand rule 3. Let's look at that rule again." Or "Watch it, now. This is where most of you goof up. Be sure to think through rule 8."

Now, for the individualized part. Some students were able to zip through the materials quickly, perhaps even skipping the first exercise. Others needed extra help with explanations and further examples before they could begin the first exercise. With no more than sixteen students at one time and taped material (which can be rewound and replayed for reinforcement or clarity), the situation permitted the lab instructor to work with every student on an individual basis without disrupting or causing others to wait. In general, during a regular class period, the lab instructor could talk individually with every student three times. If one individual needed a disproportionate amount of time, the lab instructor would leave to check on others' progress and return as often as necessary for as long as possible.

Rarely did students leave saying they had gained nothing. Obviously some gained more than others; some learn more quickly than others. Some needed to return to the lab the following day for additional reinforcement; others grasped the concept by midway through the period. The flexibility of the materials and the structure allowed the instructor to provide additional materials for those who finished early. Usually the additional materials were those that the students themselves requested, based on their own perception of needs—needs often quite different, we discovered, than those isolated by the teacher.

While I am aware of the criticism offered by some about the use of audiotapes instead of total personal contact, I find the arguments primarily philosophical. After three years of statistical work, all of which was scrutinized by both local university personnel and the state department officials who represented the federal government under which the program was funded, I feel confident in saying we really can't argue with success. The approach we used improved students' writing skills significantly, especially when we considered only those skills for which the students visited the lab. Even students in the lower levels tended to "catch up." Perhaps the secret to our success rests in the development of our own materials. Certainly we as lab instructors need not reinvent the wheel in preparing lab materials. On the other hand, if we really want to work with every student individually and there is only one of us for sixteen of them, alternatives—especially realistic, proven ones—must suffice. Students enjoyed the taped lessons, responded positively toward them, and felt free to stop, rewind, replay, or—in the cases of some who were quick to learn—advance the tape. The audio-tutorial approach allowed students the flexibility of learning at their own pace. And after all, isn't that what individualized instruction is all about?

Recommended Reading

Clark, Beverly. *Talking about Writing*. Ann Arbor: University of Michigan Press, 1985.

Elbow, Peter. *Writing without Teachers*. New York: Oxford University Press, 1973.

————. "The Loop Writing Process." In *Writing with Power*, 59–77. New York: Oxford University Press, 1981.

Graves, Richard L., ed. *Rhetoric and Composition*. Upper Montclair, N.J.: Boynton/Cook Publishers, Inc., 1983. See Murray, 89–92; Podis, 252–57.

Olson, Gary A., ed. *Writing Centers: Theory and Administration*. Urbana, Ill.: NCTE, 1984. See Bruffe, 3–14; Warnock and Warnock, 16–20; Olson, 92.

Provost, Gary. *Make Every Word Count*. Cincinnati: Writer's Digest Books, 1983.

The Writing Lab Newsletter.

13 Supervising

Elizabeth Ackley
Indian Hill High School
Cincinnati, Ohio

Survival. The pioneers of our country had to combat physical forces aimed at destruction, hostile environments, and hostile tribes, and I liken the secondary school writing center director to these pioneers for many of the same reasons. The director and the tutors must do daily battle with administrators who may or may not understand the nature and purpose of the program; students who want immediate Band-Aid surgery for papers that are due next period; students who wave a paper at a tutor and say, "I'm turning this in in five minutes and Mr. Nellis says I can have extra credit if it's signed by a writing center tutor"; fellow teachers who harumph and say that those kids helping kids can be likened to the blind leading the blind; students who become writing center groupies to avoid going to study hall; and some students who develop crushes on the tutors and invent writing assignments to get their attention. As one tutor stated, "I sometimes feel more like Dear Abby or a counselor than I do a tutor." As with those early pioneers, who discovered a new obstacle to go over, around, or through with each turn, the tutors and directors must be prepared for different problems each day—and be able to "think while standing" in order to survive.

Since the center is student based, the problems of the students dominate our concerns. The most obvious and most repeated dilemma occurs when the client expects the tutor to either do the work or patch up the paper. In order to survive with dignity and not place themselves in a position to take over the paper, my tutors never physically touch the paper of the client. I have seen some actually sit on their hands to prevent themselves from doing so, and many will not take a pen or pencil to the table so that they can reduce the temptation to do the writing for the student. They spend time explaining to the client that the thoughts and the expression of those thoughts must remain in the control and in the voice of the writer. And they begin to question, and question some more. They are much better at waiting for a response than I am. This approach usually works, especially after the center has been in operation for some time and the word spreads that the tutors will "help you write but they won't write for you."

The fine line between pointing out usage and spelling mistakes without becoming an editor varies from client to client, depending upon the expertise of the client and, yes, even the grammatical expertise of the tutor. In most situations the tutor says to the writer, "I see several misspelled words [or subject/verb disagreements, or several punctuation errors, or whatever]. Do you think you can find them? Read the paper [or the second and third lines, or the last sentence] aloud. Do you hear any errors there? If so, where? What do you think might work better?" My tutors have found the *Dictionary for Bad Spellers* (Joseph Krevisky and Jordan L. Linfield. New York: Random House, 1967), an excellent handbook for them and their clients. No tutor ever promises a "better grade" or an "A" paper. One tutor, in thinking that he admitted defeat, wrote on his record sheet, "After three full-period sessions, I realized that I was trying to make Bob's paper into an 'A' paper according to my writing standards. It simply couldn't be done." And I wrote back to him, "Right, and you shouldn't try. Take the student from where he is to as far as he can go with his paper."

Students who come to the center for other than writing help can be annoying, but in virtually every instance, I have seen my tutors handle a myriad of distractions far more calmly and effectively than I would have. One of the criteria for their selection as tutors is that they must be sensitive to other students and that includes being able to chastise them or redirect their attention. They truly do this with more aplomb than I could muster. A student's response to another student's chastisement is refreshing. The disrupter holds another student's opinion in higher regard than that of an adult's. I watched with respect and amusement as one of my tutors said in a solemn voice to a squirming and giggling seventh grader, "Haven't you learned yet that it is in extremely poor taste to laugh at your own humor?" The giggling and squirming immediately ceased and the session began.

The tutors must also be alert to the "hangers on," and, on occasion, when the groupies have been friends of the tutors, I have had to speak to the tutors and remind them of our precarious position. Teachers and administrators who see what they perceive to be "socializing" going on in the center will be quick to condemn, and, if the problem persists, rightly so.

An innovative program such as the secondary school writing center seldom wins instant or universal approval among teachers and administrators. "New" to some teachers seems synonymous with "fad," "ephemeral," or even "irresponsible" in this current buzz-word decade of "back to basics." I can only say, "Avoid confrontation, run the program as effectively as possible, and have faith that the program itself will eventually quell the criticism." And the criticism will come. Deal with each situation as professionally as possible and don't go looking for enemy tribes; let them scout you out. Find your supporters in other departments (such as social studies), and increase the number of positive troops as quietly and quickly as you can.

Most secondary school writing center directors will probably find that running the center will be an additional activity to teaching the regularly scheduled classes. Keeping track of records to justify your existence can become an endless activity, and hopefully so, because the numbers of students and the numbers of sessions should accelerate as the program becomes established. Ideally, the director will be assigned to the writing center one period per day for supervision, and this period can be used to read record sheets, respond to journals, file the record sheets, compile status reports for the administrators, check supplies, and order additional materials when needed. Whether assigned or not, I suggest that the director set aside time each day, even if after school, to keep up with the paper work. When I have allowed myself to get behind, I realized that I had lost touch with the day-to-day operation of the center, I had missed some appeals for help from the tutors on the record sheets (one client had confessed to the tutor that his mother wrote all his papers), and by the time I read it four days later, the tutor had decided that I approved by my lack of immediate response. I have not fallen behind in my daily reading of record sheets since then.

The expected and hidden risks in pioneering are myriad, but survival can be a reality if the tutors are carefully selected, the director has a handle on the concept and the purpose of the center, the tutors understand and can implement that concept and purpose, and the program itself can quell the enemy by its continued growth and increasing support by the students and the other teachers in the school.

14 Keeping Records in the Writing Lab

Anne Wright
Hazelwood West High School
Hazelwood, Missouri

"How many students came to the writing lab last year? How many hours did you spend actually tutoring? Are those computers really being used?" These are the kinds of questions we anticipated being asked when we started our writing lab at Hazelwood West High School. By anticipating the need to justify our existence with records and by supplying them before we were asked, we have been able to maintain our lab and add new services.

Occasionally there are times during a particular day when no students are in the lab, so a principal who walks in during one of those periods is likely to wonder whether the money we spend on the facility and staff is earning an adequate return. Fortunately, we have the records to prove that we serve a sufficient number of students to be cost effective. Of course, we know that real effectiveness is not represented by numbers but by the availability and quality of a service never before offered to our students. But these days, when accountability is the byword, we have to offer concrete evidence.

We begin our record keeping when a student walks in the door. Students are supposed to bring referral forms from the teachers who sent them to the writing lab. This form, which is on NCR paper, has the student's name, teacher's name, course title, room number, class hour, description of the assignment the student is to work on, date, and time the student left the classroom. At the end of the hour, the lab staff member fills in the lower portion of the form with a summary of the session. There is also a place to check whether the assignment was completed or not, and, if not, how many more class periods may be needed to complete it. We file the originals of these forms in student folders, which we keep for every student. The second copy is returned to the classroom teacher at the end of the school day. If the student needs to return for another session, we staple a pass to the form so the teacher will not have to bother with that the next time. Now that the lab has been open for enough years that the students are well aware of its existence and what it can offer, we have many self-referrals who simply come in with hall passes from the teachers who excused them. In these cases, we do not fill out referral sheets.

When students first come to the writing lab, a staff member hands them an information sheet to fill out, asking for name, parents' names, address, phone number, class referred or excused from, and grade level. At the bottom of the sheet, there is a place for the staff member who works with the student to fill out after the session. We mark the kind of work we do with the students as remedial, enrichment, developmental, or contest (if they come to find information about writing contests or to seek help in entering one). We also indicate what kind of paper the student is writing: paragraph, multiparagraph, research, critical paper, or other kind.

While students fill out the top portion of the form, we write their names on the tab of a file folder and on a sheet we call the *Daily Log*. On this, in addition to the student's name, we record the name of the referral teacher and the class period. The major portion of the page is divided into three sections, one labeled *Date*, one *Problems Worked On*, the third *Specific Recommendations for Work During Next Session*. The lab staff member fills in this section after working with the student. Both the information sheet and the daily log are filed in the student's folder, which we keep in a file cabinet. Each time that student returns to the lab, we update the daily log.

Originally, we used the names and addresses to send letters to the parents of every new student who came to the writing lab. We were offering a new service, and we wanted the parents to know about it. Now that we are in our fourth year of operation, we have discontinued that practice, not because we have decided it wasn't a sound idea and excellent publicity for the school, but simply because the paper work grew beyond our ability to keep up with it. Even though we had a form letter on NCR paper (we kept one copy in the student's folder), we still wrote personal messages on each one; if we had five or six students per hour for several class periods, the letters became a real burden. The letters occasionally brought telephone calls from parents who thanked us for helping their sons or daughters or asked for more information about the lab. As I write this, recalling the responses we received, I wonder if we shouldn't reinstate the practice of sending letters in spite of the time problem because they did seem to result in positive parental attitudes.

In our first year of operation, we asked students to fill out evaluation forms before they left the lab, but we had to abandon that idea quickly because there simply wasn't enough time to do the evaluation. Now we occasionally give teachers some evaluation forms and ask them to have these filled out by any students who have been to the lab. We also give teachers evaluation forms at the end of each year.

In our lab, we also keep "sign-up" and "sign-in-and-out" sheets. When teachers know they are going to send students to the lab or when they want to bring a whole class, they sign up ahead of time on weekly sign-up sheets we keep just inside the door for their convenience. If students come in who have not been previously signed up, we add their names to the sign-up sheet. We keep these sheets on file so that, if there is ever any question about a student's having been in the lab or about the accuracy of our reports, or even about one or two teachers dominating the use of the lab, we have our records to examine. We also ask individual students who come in to sign their names on another sheet and write the time they come in and the time they will leave; this way, teachers can check on whether the students were here when they were supposed to be. This is unneccessary, of course, when a teacher brings a whole class to the lab.

In order to be able to classify the kinds of information we gather from students, we use the PFS File, Sort, and Report software programs. During the first two years, we printed monthly reports to give to teachers, the communications department chair, and the principal. For the last two years, we have just printed semester reports. No one seemed especially interested in the monthly reports, and preparing them took time away from working with students.

Our reports contain the following information:

Total students tutored individually _____
Total students who came to the lab with a whole class _____
Total students who were in classes for which the lab staff did classroom presentations on how to write a particular kind of paper _____

Total individual tutoring hours _____
Total hours with students in whole classes
    (the number of students in each class multiplied by the number of hours the class spent in the lab) _____
Total clock hours in classroom demonstrations _____

The above three categories are added to get:
    total hours with students _____

Number of contest entries _____

Then we break those data down into a chart that lists the teachers who sent students to the lab and what department they are in, the number of students they sent, and how many hours the staff spent tutoring students for each teacher who is listed.

Next, we categorize how many students came from each course and how many total hours we tutored students from those courses. Then we list how many students were categorized as remedial, developmental, enrichment, or contest. Another way we group the statistics is by the number of students in each grade who have been to the writing lab. We also list the teachers' classes for which we have provided classroom demonstrations. We list teachers who have brought whole classes to the lab and how many total hours we spent with them.

The last part of our report consists of listings of the names of students who have used the writing lab. We categorize these names in several different ways: by the referral teacher and the total hours spent in the lab; by the grade level; by classification as to remedial, developmental, enrichment, or contest; by student names with referral teachers and number of hours spent in the lab; by courses students have been referred from.

Finally, we print a list of all teachers who referred students to the lab and how many tutoring hours were spent with each teacher's students.

In addition to these records, we also have the usual kind of library card records of which teachers have checked out books from our professional library. (We maintain a collection of approximately seventy-five books and other kinds of resource materials on teaching writing.) We also keep a bibliography of these materials on a computer disk and update it as we buy new resource materials or books. We print this bibliography once or twice a year to distribute to teachers.

To help the staff keep its perspective on how well we are fulfilling our mission, we use all of the information we gather through the means I've described to write a year-end report each spring. We attach to this report a list of goals for the next year. We give copies to our department chair and principal, but these reports serve mainly to help us take a critical look at our program and see where we need to make changes and what additional services we need to offer.

This process of record keeping must sound formidable, but it really doesn't take too much time away from working with students in the lab. Once the routine is established, the process works smoothly. We have one English teacher and a teacher assistant in the writing lab all day, and the teacher assistant does most of the record keeping. Our assistant happens to be very efficient and fast; maybe the task would seem more intimidating if we didn't have such good help. But accurate, complete record keeping is worth the time and effort for programs such as writing labs because, if a money crunch comes along, such programs will be the first ones considered for cutting.[1] If you have the records to prove the value of your program, you are much more likely to keep that program.

Notes

1. As Sharon Sorenson has observed: "Without the aide, the writing lab's smooth operation would never become a fact. Chaos, perhaps, but not a smooth operation. What she [Sharon's lab aide] did, allowed us to have meaningful instructional time with students during every lab visit semester after semester. What she did allowed us to have suitable materials when none existed. What she did allowed us to develop the public relations we needed to survive. . . .

"An aide offers significant services at a cost considerably reduced from that of the lab instructor. Sure, the lab instructor can complete those student records. Sure, the lab instructor can make copies of those records and forward them to the teachers involved each day. Sure, the lab instructor can type and duplicate and collate and file and sort. Sure, the lab instructor can prepare, copy, and complete menial public relations responsibilities. But that's expensive clerical help. And it's expensive in two ways: not only is a fully licensed, experienced English teacher paid too much to be a clerk, but the time for which she is being paid is not being spent doing what she does most effectively: teaching students. Sure, most teachers can type, file, collate, and staple. Heaven knows they do enough of it. But if a lab instructor is responsible for the entire operation of a lab for an entire school, then an aide is a must. She is a must both physically and financially, both for students and staff. It's obvious what happens without her. Either the lab operation is, if not chaos, then seriously inefficient, or the lab instructor must devote major blocks of time doing what an aide could do far more inexpensively. And either case is to the detriment of the lab's single purpose, to tutor students on an individual basis.

"When the response is, 'We can't afford an aide,' the reply ought to be, 'We can't afford *not* to have an aide.' "

III Computers and Other Equipment

The majority of writing centers/labs have computers, according to the results of my survey. That reality becomes more obvious each day as schools add computers to existing facilities or donate "antiquated" equipment to the English department when new hardware has been purchased. Chapter 15 focuses on equipment used at the Hazelwood West High School Writing Lab, with emphasis on the computer and problems with the changes from older to newer models. Over the past five years, I have worked with several groups of English instructors to learn with them and then teach others how to use computers for teaching writing. Writing centers/labs use these computers to improve writing in ways that are described in Chapter 17, but they also use them for computer assisted instruction and as part of an interaction between writer and tutor, as discussed in Chapter 16. Though I feel strongly that computers should not be used as learning machines to replace teachers of writing, I do believe that we should listen to a voice such as that in Chapter 18, to find out how CAI can be integrated into the teaching of writing in a writing center. If a writing center/lab is a place for writing and working on writing, then perhaps there is a need for some CAI software for the student who wants that kind of reinforcement. On the other hand, I feel just as strongly that computers with word-processing software should be used as part of an interaction between writer and tutor.—The Editor

15 Equipment for the Writing Lab/Center

Anne Wright
Hazelwood West High School
Hazelwood, Missouri

To paraphrase the old saying about education, all you really need in order to have a writing lab is a teacher on one end of a log and a student on the other. However, it helps if you have a few materials, some equipment, and more than one teacher. What we have in our lab at Hazelwood West High School goes far beyond basic necessities. I can't emphasize too much, however, that it is not necessary to have any special equipment or resources to get started. If you can get released time for a teacher to work with students individually, seize the opportunity and don't worry about what you don't have. Once you get started, you can always try to add staff, order supplies, buy equipment, or improve your facilities. If you wait to start until your school district is willing to give you everything, you may never have a writing lab.

Once a teacher has been given released time, the next step is to find a suitable place for the lab. Depending on whether you are to work primarily through the English department, as we are, or whether you are to serve all departments equally, you will want to choose a place that is accessible and visible to the clientele. The first two years that we had a lab, it was separated from the English department by a long hall. We felt that the distance prevented teachers from sending as many students to the lab as they might otherwise have done. Last year we moved into a new facility in a corner of our library, across the hall from the English classrooms. Students and teachers both seem more aware of our presence and use the lab more often.

No equipment is necessary for starting, but a computer or two can be very helpful since word processing can be a great motivator for writing. We started with one Apple IIe, a dual disk drive, and an Epson printer. Both the lab staff and the students learned to use the equipment during the first year. The second year we had six computers, two of which had dual disk drives, four Epson printers, and an NEC Spinwriter (letter-quality) printer. By the time we moved in the fall of 1985, we had ten Apple IIe's and seven printers. At the present time, we have twenty-four stationary computers (all Apple IIe's) and eleven printers (the same Spinwriter, some Epson MXs, some Epson LXs, and one Epson FX). We also have a computer, disk drive, and monitor on a portable cart to be used with a large-screen monitor on another cart. These units can be checked out by teachers for use in classroom instruction. Fifteen of our computers have 128K, and I would advise anyone purchasing computers now to be sure that their computers have at least that same capability. However, we are not having any problems with our original 64K machines.

If you have computers, buying software is the next step. You need to choose wisely because there is so much available now and much of the software will not be very helpful. We no longer buy usage, punctuation, or grammar programs because the few we have do not get used. We use the Apple Writer II word-processing program and find it very easy for high school students to learn, and yet powerful enough to perform many of the sophisticated functions they may need for their papers (such as using superscripting and subscripting in research papers).

However, since computer use has grown so rapidly in the past few years, we have had some problems. Apple has changed its DOS (disk operating system) from 3.3 to 2.0 (ProDos). Our programs are 3.3, which Apple does not produce any more, so we cannot replace them. To buy additional disks for our new computers, we have to buy the ProDos version of Apple Writer. ProDos does not work exactly the same way as Dos, and it is more complicated for students to use. Not that the students can't learn to do it—but most of them already know the 3.3 version. This is an example of the unforeseen kinds of problems you can run into when you deal with a developing technology. We continue to use the 3.3 disks, but we know, that when those disks wear out, we will have to retrain our students.

Other software that you will find useful includes a spelling checker (we use Sensible Speller by the Sensible Software Company) and a graphics program (we have Print Shop). In addition to these, we also have Newsroom, and Apple Works, and PFS File, Sort, and Report for record keeping. The first two are used by journalism and modern media classes and by some teachers. Students who know those programs already come in occasionally to use them.

Accessories that you will need for your computers include a supply of disks and boxes to store them in. You will also need paper for your printers. Letter-quality printers should be loaded with heavier paper than that which is used for dot-matrix printers. Tables for the computer components are another essential. A separate table for each computer unit (comprising keyboard and CPU, disk drive, monitor, and printer) is desirable. But we have two units on some tables. Tables with wheels are especially helpful because you can move the units around to gain access to wall plugs. Multiple electrical strips are very convenient, although you can get along without them if you have an electrical wall strip or many, many wall receptacles. We use one multiple strip of six outlets for each unit.

Because we do not have one printer for each computer, we have printer interface boxes to which two or more computers can be plugged in. The box enables us to switch on the printer from either computer. These boxes are available to serve two, three, four, and perhaps more computers. We assign one printer to every two computers to ensure that we have time to get all students' work printed within the class hour.

I've written many words about computers, here, because they are an integral part of our writing lab. But I want to state once more that they are not a requirement for a tutoring lab. In fact, because we have so many computers, we have to try very hard to keep from becoming a computer lab instead of a writing lab. We feel it is crucial to maintain our identity as a tutoring center because our students need more help with writing than they do with computers.

With that thought in mind, let me tell you what other equipment we have that can be useful, with or without computers. The main piece of equipment is an electric typewriter. We still find uses for it, in spite of all the computers we have available. You'll also want plenty of bulletin board space for displaying student writing and announcements about writing contests. A teacher's desk, some tables and chairs for students, and bookcases, a storage cabinet, and a file cabinet will all be useful. However, you could get by with a table and several chairs for the teacher and students to use together.

In our writing lab we have gathered two kinds of materials. We have one bookcase full of textbooks used in our composition courses, literature books used in our literature courses, dictionaries, thesauruses, style books, pamphlets on special writing problems, and file folders of suggestions for taking essay tests, writing resumes, and getting started on a paper. In our other bookcase, we keep materials that can be used by English teachers or any other interested teachers. These materials include approximately seventy-five books on teaching writing as well as collections of periodicals that relate to writing, for which the lab has subscriptions. Every month we receive a class set (thirty copies) of *Writing* and one copy each of the *English Journal,* the *Quarterly* of the National Writing Project and Center for the Study of Writing, *Computers, Reading, and Language Arts,* and *The Computing Teacher.* These materials are available for teachers to check out.

Because our school board and administration have been so generous in buying equipment and supplies for us, we have what we consider a rather luxurious lab. But all of the staff members feel, I believe, that we were performing a much-needed service even in our first year, when we didn't have much more than the log sitters. The most important ingredient is the teacher with the desire to help students learn to communicate their ideas clearly in writing. If your school will pay for that teacher, you can open for business.

16 Computers Interact with Writers and Tutors

Pamela B. Farrell
Red Bank Regional High School
Little Silver, New Jersey

I have observed something unique in the relationship between tutors and writers in our writing center. Tutors and writers, all of whom are high school students in grades 9–12, have varying social, educational, and ethnic backgrounds; yet when they are working together in front of the computer, all differences vanish and a new relationship develops. As Dawn, a tutor explains, "Once you are able to put aside all the unimportant stuff and learn to trust one another, then I don't think background really matters."[1] Another tutor comments, "I think variety [in backgrounds] is very important because you not only give to someone what you have experienced and what you know, but you also get from them a new viewpoint or a new perspective, a different opinion, a new idea." Students see the computer acting as a third party or as neutral ground that encourages collaboration, provides immediate feedback and ease in revision, invites more writing, opens a dialogue between writer and tutor, acts as a learning device, and allows writers to take pride in their work. If the computer does, in fact, interact with writer and tutor in these ways, what more could we as writing center directors want? By looking at some examples of each of these kinds of interaction, perhaps we can learn how to encourage more of what is already happening between writer, tutor, and computer.

The experience of working with a writer at the computer is an unusual one. Terry, a gregarious honors student and tutor, describes the difference when working with a writer at the computer:

> There's a big difference because when it's [the writing is] on the screen, . . . you're both looking at it. . . . You can both look for errors and not feel that it's the student's paper because you are both looking to fix the printout on the screen. . . . It's a third party. . . . When you have a class look for grammatical errors, it's

much easier to do than if it's someone else's writing or something
that's not close to you. The screen sort of gives you some distance.

He is right. Dave, a writer who also has become a tutor, says that,
when writers see their work on the monitor, they get the idea that "I
didn't do it, you didn't do it, the computer did it. And the computer
can't talk back to you, so you can attack it!" The monitor becomes
neutral ground where writer and tutor can work on a clean copy that
they can both read. Even the writers are aware of the difference as
Jay, a writer with minimum basic skills, comments, "I was able to see
clearly what I was writing and I could benefit from the help of others."

Collaboration has become the key word as students share work on
the monitor, share problems with writing, collaborate on revision and
ideas from prewriting to final drafts. After working together with tutor
Dave, Rob says, "Dave and I could see the work on the screen; we
could see what was going on; we could see where to change punctuation, where to change words if any needed to be changed, and you
know that's a lot better than writing on paper." Tutor Michele admits
that "helping others with their writing skills [on the computer] has
helped me to look at my papers critically." One of our frequent visitors
for two years has been Walter, a dysgraphic student.[2] When Walter
has asked him how to spell words, Dave encourages Walter to "just
type it out on the computer and see if it looks right" before going to
the dictionary. Dave believes that on the computer "you say the words
and spell them out in your mind, and you'll see it on the screen and
you also hear yourself saying it. So it really helped him [Walter] spell
words better."

Collaboration is just one way in which the computer has helped
Walter. As our tutor Dawn reported, the immediate feedback which
Walter received by seeing his work appear in neat form on the monitor
"gave him that lift that he often needed to be positive about his
writing . . . and it gave him a feeling that he belonged, that he wasn't
different from other students." Walter is not alone; Rob, a creative
writing major, describes how the computer "just makes it [my writing]
right there where you can see it. You can see what's going on and
sometimes that's better than when you're writing—you can see everything you've written already up on the screen." Not only do writers
see their work immediately, with and without mistakes, but they know
how easy it is to improve what they have written. Terry explains,
"What the computer helps do is go from what you might bring out
of tutoring as a good or strong paper to a really good paper, you know,
changing a B to a B+ or a B+ to an A−, adding that little difference
there." Some people, however, just come to the writing center when

they have to write a formal paper. Jessica, for instance, admits that
the main reason she uses the computer is that " it's so much easier
than the typewriter." Others indicate that the ease of revision "makes
you more willing to change things around knowing that you don't
have to waste paper, you don't have to erase, and it's fun."

With the encouragement of the tutor, writers tend to do more writing
on the computers. Last year a writer remarked, "I've written over
twenty long poems since using the computer. Without it, I probably
would have written only three. Every time I sit in front of the computer,
I somehow manage to work out and write down at least a rough idea
that otherwise might be lost in my questionable memory." Dawn senses
that you don't have the classroom atmosphere of writing at a desk
when you are sitting at the computer, "so the writer who oftentimes
can't think of anything to write may come up with some great ideas
at the computer." Another tutor believes that "students write more
when they can write on the computer, and they save it all together
so they don't have to worry about a paper being lost or ripped or
anything like that." Those of us who have lost files on the computer
may not consider those losses significant, but one of our tutors thinks
a writer's loss of a file is important because "I've done the same thing,
and it's shared pain!"

Once the tutor and writer can share an experience at the computer,
the dialogue begins. Tutors have made me aware of a technique I refer
to as the "computer ploy." Writers use the excuse of not knowing how
to do something on the computer; then the tutor discovers that "the
questions were really about writing and not about the computer."
Another tutor found that "they [the writers] will want to underline,
but before they do that they want to know what you think or how
this reads, so they usually have another motive behind their question."
Some tutors enjoy the opportunity of getting to know a writer by
working at the computer. For instance, one admits that he does "weird
things" at the computer because "it's very easy to get to know someone
when you're working at the computer." That dialogue frequently
focuses on developing the writing through questioning. Dawn describes
how she is able to get information out of the writer by looking at the
monitor and the writing. While they sit eye to eye at the monitor, she
asks the writers how they feel about the assignment and if they have
any idea about what they want to say. Then the computer seems to
act as a catalyst for opening the dialogue necessary for an effective
tutor-writer relationship.

Invariably a tutor must play the role of instructor. Our tutors are
trained to be readers/listeners. The computer serves as a learning

device that both the writer and tutor profit from in this interaction. Dana, a senior, explains that when she put something on the monitor "I would ask them [the tutors] if they would help me construct the sentence better or add a different word that would sound better." Although many teachers would suggest that Dana refer to a thesaurus or grammar book instead, the computer becomes the means by which Dana and the tutor may question grammatical structure or word choice; they may, in fact, look in a thesaurus or grammar book for reinforcement, and they will probably remember what they have learned! This experience also teaches the tutor to apply the lessons learned. One tutor notes, "As a peer tutor, I get to see how others write, observe what they've done right and wrong. I then use this [knowledge] to better my own writing."

Finally, one of the most important, unexpected benefits of the interaction between the writer and tutor working at the computer is the pride writers develop in their efforts. Some of our brightest days have been the ones in which advanced placement students and basic skills students alike have successfully completed a piece of writing and printed a neat, legible copy to share. Several of the tutors and I remember the first time our dysgraphic student wrote and printed out something. One recalls, "He was so proud of himself and so proud of his work that . . . [the computer] really made a difference!"

Does the computer make a difference in the interaction between writer and tutor? Yes, but I would be lying if I said that my opinion hasn't been influenced significantly by the interaction of the peer tutors who act as readers/listeners. In any writing center, the director depends on an outstanding team of trained tutors who create the kind of atmosphere in which writers grow, share, collaborate, and enjoy writing. If the computer adds another element to that atmosphere, then why not use it to its full potential as part of the interaction between writer and tutor.

Notes

1. The interviews were taped January 22–23, 1986, and February 26, 1986, in the writing center at Red Bank Regional High School.

2. *The Dictionary of Reading and Learning Disabilities Terms* defines dysgraphia as the "inability to perform the required motor tasks for handwriting and, thus, the power to express ideas by writing."

17 Revising Aids: A Step Beyond Word Processing

Pat Stoddart
Logan High School
Logan, Utah

The computerized writing center at Logan High School is not a referral lab, but one that is fully integrated into the English curriculum. Junior and senior students work in the writing center for one-fourth of their English instruction time.

The "Writing Room," originally a grade-school media center, houses twenty-four IBM PCs, five letter-quality printers, and conferencing tables spaced strategically throughout the room. A full-time aide handles the scheduling for the room, maintenance for the hardware, and filing of software programs and student disks. She also gives all the basic instruction on word processing.

To help compose process writing assignments, the students use WANDAH, a software program originally titled "Writer's Aid and Author's Helper"—now marketed by Harcourt Brace Jovanovich as "HBJ Writer."

All Logan High English teachers teach writing as a process, using the computerized lab to support the philosophy and activities in their classrooms. The writing assignments, designed and written by the teachers, correlate with the standards of the Utah State core curriculum. A student who is assigned a typical composition, like "A Moment" paper, spends approximately five to eight class periods working on the composition. The models for the assignments are the selections used for literary study in the class. In *To Kill A Mockingbird*, Scout's narrative moments reveal the form for the students' own narrative papers.

For each writing assignment that students complete, they move through a process similar to the one William Strong envisions (figure 1).

Prewriting activities, such as adding sensory details or performing a piece of classroom drama demonstrating "showing, not telling," help students with techniques for more effective writing. Students also participate in warm-up and discovery activities before they begin drafting

111

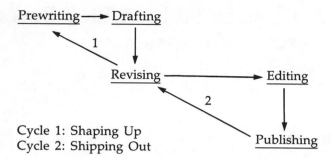

Cycle 1: Shaping Up
Cycle 2: Shipping Out

Fig. 1. The writing process revisited.
(Source: Strong 1986, 2. Used with permission.)

their papers. Most of the prewriting occurs in the classroom before students go to "The Writing Room." However, WANDAH does have four prewriting activities that do, sometimes, help students at this stage: "Nutshelling," "Planning," "Freewriting" and "Invisible Writing."

"Nutshelling" and "Planning" are short aids that can help students think about an expository piece of writing. Students are asked to address purpose and audience and to write a thesis. The "Freewriting" and "Invisible Writing" aids rest on Peter Elbow's theory of the power of brainstorming, where no one, not even the writer, is allowed to criticize or revise while ideas are flowing (1973, 5). WANDAH's "Freewriting" aid flashes a signal to the hesitant writer—"Just keep typing." For the "Invisible Writer," the screen goes blank; the students write one hundred words before they can see what they have written. Both of these programs do not allow revising, thus teaching the concept of noncritical brainstorming. Students use these aids during any part of the process when they are stymied and need to look inside their heads for new ideas.

Once students are in the lab, they draft either the conventional way at tables or at computers. After the first draft is completed, they work in response groups for content and organizational strategies. Another program that WANDAH has, which students use during the first cycle of Strong's process, is "Commenting." This program was devised for peer review and allows one student to comment on another student's disk without changing the original composition. The reviewer's comments are underlined and appear inside the text. The writer can then decide whether or not to incorporate the reviewer's comments into the original composition. Throughout the process, students are free to move from computers to tables to response groups, collaborating and revising to complete pre-edited drafts.

For a process writing assignment, students do most of the writing on WANDAH's word processor. The revising section of the program adds an analysis, allowing for specific stylistic or editing types of instruction related to students' own pieces of writing. Only in the second cycle of the process—revising, editing and publishing—do students use WANDAH's revising aids; these programs help writers "clean-up" a piece of writing. Work on word usage, active verbs, or spelling becomes appropriate only after students have interesting ideas that are effectively arranged. Even then, teachers do not use all the revising aids for one writing experience. Teaching stylistic techniques such as avoiding strings of prepositional phrases and using active verbs, at the same time, would confuse high school writers. Also, the stylistic principle should match the kind of writing the student is working on. Avoiding strings of prepositions is more appropriate for expository writing than narrative, for example.

Most of the revising aids need teacher instruction for students to see how these aids apply to their own writing. However, the spelling, word choice, and mechanics aids need little instruction to be effective. These aids simply highlight a possible mistake such as a missed quotation mark or a misuse of the word "their." The spelling checker program marks any words that are not in the WANDAH dictionary and makes the writer decide whether or not the spelling is correct. In all of these programs, the students can correct the errors as they find them on the screen because the revising program is fully integrated with WANDAH's word processor.

For the other revising aids, teachers design specific activities to teach the concept that governs the aid. For each "Writing Room" process writing assignment, only one or two of these aids are integrated into the process. For example, for "The Moment" paper, students get a hard-copy printout of their pre-edited compositions with all the "to be" verbs marked. They return to the classroom for instruction on creating more powerful sentences by using active verbs. After a short demonstration, students use their own writing to practice the concept. Students, working with their own writing, seem to learn stylistics, usage, and mechanical principles of writing much more readily and permanently than they do working out of textbooks with someone else's isolated, uninteresting sentences.

Two of the revising aids, a "Sentence Outline" and a "Transition Search," can help teach organizational strategies. For the "Sentence Outline," the computer marks either the first sentence of a paragraph, or a selected topic sentence within the paragraph, and produces an outline of the paper. Obviously, this aid is appropriate for only a few, very specific kinds of writing.

The "Transition Search" marks common transition words and phrases, such as "first," "later," "in addition," and "for example." In the classroom, teachers can use student writing to show how transitions can establish relationships between ideas. Most of the time, the lesson on using transitions is made visible by the scarcity of marked words in a student's composition, so the transition search aid is of little value without interpretation and clarification.

The "Pronoun Search" also helps give the teacher and student meaningful classroom material for working on such common problems in usage as pronoun agreement and clear pronoun references. Instruction can focus on problems individual students have using pronouns. Mina Shaughnessy says teachers should "heighten the student's awareness of the grammar web he spins as he moves from left to right across the page" (1977, 114). She says this can be done by having students draw a line from each pronoun to its antecedent or between two pronouns to call attention to any shifts in person. This exercise is more easily accomplished when the computer marks the pronouns so students can identify a pronoun and see how it works in the composition.

Three additional aids, "Abstract," "-tion," and "Gender-Specific" word searches, identify words that carry vague or inaccurate meanings. From these aids, students can develop an awareness of the value of specific word choice. When, in students' own papers, a word such as "beauty" is highlighted as an abstract word, or "relation" as a weak noun, they will benefit from lessons on adding exact details and using strong verbs to replace general nouns.

When the computer identifies, again in their own papers, gender-specific nouns, such as "policeman," "manmade" and "stewardess" as sexist words, students see that language often carries unintended messages. Showing such students words like "police officer," "synthetic" and "flight attendant" as alternatives without bias suggests more than one word replacing another. It alerts them to the changing and complex nature of language.

Students learn the stylistic principle of avoiding strings of prepositional phrases for concise, clear and rhythmic writing best by manipulating their own created sentences. For a classroom activity on revising strings of prepositional phrases, students could revise a sentence like, "The game for the championship in baseball took place in the spring at the end of the season in Salt Lake City." The student who wrote the sentence might change it to, "The championship game in Salt Lake City ended the baseball season."

The most effective stylistic aid for high school students is the "To Be" find, another word search program where all the verbs are marked. The principle behind this program is easy for students to understand. For example, students immediately see the animation that occurs by simply replacing "is" with "hung" in the sentence, "The fog is on the valley." They can see the result of changing passive to active voice ("The test was failed" to "They failed the test") and using active verbs instead of linking verbs ("Grandpa's voice was frightening to the child" to "Grandpa's voice frightened the child"). Students more effectively internalize all of the stylistic changes when they practice them in the context of their own writing.

Varying sentence structure is another stylistic technique that is taught by WANDAH's revising aids. The sentence length graph displays a graph of the number of words per sentence and the number of sentences in each paragraph. A graph that displays short sentences may indicate choppy, disjointed thoughts (figure 2). One that has long sentences may be confusing and boring to the reader (figure 3).

The stylistic principle of sentence variety is best taught with sentence combining activities used during the editing-revising stage of the process. Playing with different sentence structures improves students' skills in constructing clear, smooth and effective sentences. After students have worked through some "closure" and "open" exercises in sentence combining (Strong 1984) and then rewrite some of their own sentences, they have the computer make a new graph displaying the variety of the sentences in the revised draft (figure 4).

Although Ruth Von Blum, the author of WANDAH, created the sentence length graph to prompt writers into using a variety of sentence lengths, for high school students it serves another purpose. When a student's graph shows sentences more than forty words long, the teacher is alerted to a potential problem with run-on sentences and can group together students with this problem in order to give special attention to those who need it.

WANDAH is not the only computer program that contains prewriting and revising aids, although it is the only one with an integrated word processor. Available for the Apple and IBM, William Wresch's Writer's Helper, published by Conduit, works with any of the Apple or IBM word processors; students use two computer programs. Writer's Helper

----+---10----+---20

Paragraph 1
lllllll
llllllll
llllllll
llllll
lllll
llllll
llll

Fig. 2. Sentence length graph (shorter).

----+---10----+---20----+---30----+---40----+---50-

Paragraph 1
llllllllllllllllllllllllllllllllllllllllllllllllllllllll
lllllllllllllll
Paragraph 2
llllllllllllllllllllll
llllllllllllllllllllllllllllllllllll
llllllllllllllllllllllllllllllllll
lllllllllllllllllllll
lllllllllllllllllllllll
lllll
llllllllllllllllllllll

Fig. 3. Sentence length graph (longer).

----+---10----+---20----+

Paragraph 1
lllllllllllll
lllllllllllllllllllll
lll
llllllll
llllllllllllllll

Fig. 4. Sentence length graph (after revision).

has many of the same revising features WANDAH has and many more prewriting aids. The prewriting part of Writer's Helper contains eleven prewriting activities for students to do at the computer. Many of these, such as "The Questioner" and "Three Ways of Seeing," are simply programmed sets of heuristics that ask students generic questions, helping to steer them in the direction of choosing a topic or developing one.

These activities, although they could be done as efficiently without a computer, are often helpful the first few times, but students quickly resist answering the same sets of questions for different writing assignments. Wresch has unique ideas; for example, he compares something to a day-old meatloaf, and interesting computer interpretations of traditional techniques for getting students to think about their subjects. However, prewriting activities, such as those he has incorporated into his computer program, thrive on verbal exchange of ideas, and the classroom provides a more natural setting for this to happen.

A new collegiate version of Writer's Workbench is now available for the AT&T personal computer. Working with an AT&T word processor, this program has no prewriting aids but includes several additional revising aids, such as "Frequently Misused Words and Phrases," "Split Infinitives" and "A Sentence Analysis" (Kinkead 1986).

Each program has some advantages over others. The English Department at Logan High uses WANDAH because it was the pilot school during the development of the program at UCLA. Since all students and teachers use WANDAH, one of its most important features has been the ease with which students learn to use it. However, it is not the merits of an individual computer program that help students find success in writing, but the teaching philosophy that governs the use of a program. Computers profit teachers who work through the process of writing a composition with their students and who focus their instruction on the students' own writing. Students who practice process writing and receive meaningful, individual instruction become discerning writers and thinkers.

References

Elbow, Peter. *Writing Without Teachers*. New York: Oxford University Press, 1973.

Kinkead, Joyce. "Matching Software and Curriculum: A Description of Four Text-Analysis Programs." *Computers and Composition* August 1986: 33–55.

Shaughnessy, Mina P. *Errors and Expectations.* New York: Oxford University Press, 1977.

Strong, William. *Creative Approaches to Sentence Combining.* Urbana, Ill.: ERIC/ NCTE, 1986.

Strong, William. *Practicing Sentence Options.* New York: Random House, 1984.

18 Why Computer Assisted Instruction?

Betty Barbara Sipe
Mt. Lebanon Senior High School
Pittsburgh, Pennsylvania

> Tell me, I forget.
> Show me, I remember.
> Involve me, I understand.
>
> —Ancient Chinese Proverb

Students involved in Computer Assisted Instruction (CAI) are learning the truth of this age-old adage. Software that runs the gamut from avoiding fragments to writing complete and well-structured sentences, from outlining procedures to writing multi-paragraph papers, and from simplified word study and spelling to preparation for a Scholastic Aptitude Test (SAT) challenge and encourage students at their individual achievement levels. In "The Write Place" at Mt. Lebanon Senior High School, students discover how CAI helps to eliminate weaknesses and build strengths in their written communication. [Note that, in all cases, the CAI complements the work done by the classroom teacher and/or the writing center/lab person.]

Computer Assisted Instruction merits applause first for its positive approach to helping students overcome weaknesses in their use of the English language. Built into every software program are plaudits for work done correctly; and, if students fail to answer correctly, the computer neither castigates nor demeans them in any way. Rather, the software encourages students to try again, soldering the relationship between the operator and the computer and serving as a centrifugal force that encourages achievement. Therefore, the fear of failure is eradicated from the students' minds when they use CAI for remediation, reinforcement, or enrichment.

CAI's capability to give program users immediate feedback adds still another dimension to students' willingness to be challenged; and this often proves not only challenging but also enjoyable. Several students who had difficulty with sentence fragments used Sentences

119

and Fragments, which arrived about the time of the opening baseball game in Pittsburgh. The students were ecstatic when they heard the melodious strains of "Take Me Out to the Ball Game" every time they had a correct answer! Although this was a very basic lesson on the subject and predicate of a sentence and on the sentence fragment, nevertheless it caused the students to exclaim, "All right! Hey, that's pretty neat!"

In addition, CAI helps when I work with groups of students with varying levels of ability on "noodle networking," my name for a frugal kind of networking practiced in "The Write Place." Working with four students at each computer or an entire class grouped around the lab's four Apple IIe computers, I start a discussion on a single- or multi-paragraph paper that has been saved on the computer. Students then consider the merits of the paper, the questions that arise from lack of clarity or completeness of thoughts, and the suggestions for improvement. Frequently, I need do little, if anything, to get them to consider the plaudits of the paper first and to keep our discussion progressing. "Student Activities" in the user's handbook of The Bank Street Writer includes simplified lessons that can be modified for more advanced students and used with this kind of critical analysis. In addition, the activities include practice in using transitional elements, striving for clarity, combining sentences, developing standards for writing, studying verb tense, examining logical sentence order, and so forth. One time, for example, when students from a modified composition course visited the writing lab to learn about the use of the active voice, I had previously programmed a paragraph into the computer, based on a lesson in the "Student Activities" section, that included "blah verbs" (forms of the verb "to be") and the passive voice. After students were grouped around the Apple IIe computers, the four operators retrieved the file and then all of the students read the entire paragraph before the discussion began. Although some students were a little reticent and reluctant to comment when the discussion started, all students became actively involved during the session. The comments they made as they left the lab proved the impact CAI had on them. They expressed an interest in returning to the lab during their study halls or before or after school to work on software that would help them to improve their skills in the writing process. For their more advanced students, teachers can select passages for CAI that challenge these students.

CAI also provides reinforcement for students who need supplementary aids to develop particular skills in written communication. This is true of Computer Assisted Writing (CAW), which offers students assistance in writing a business letter of complaint, a report, and a persuasive composition. The tutorial part of the software that deals with a persuasive composition, for example, begins with a sentence-by-sentence breakdown of a model introductory paragraph, giving the specific purpose of each sentence. Students read the model paragraph and then answer the questions about the "intended" audience and the "opinion" of the paragraph. Next, students choose a topic from a "Topic Menu" and write an introduction. Prompts encourage the students to be sure that each sentence serves its defined purpose. Students also can have their completed paragraphs analyzed in order to make additions or corrections. Once students have completed their own introductory paragraphs to their satisfaction, they follow similar tutorial steps for writing two body paragraphs and a conclusion. In this way, the students gain self-confidence while writing a persuasive composition.

For students intent on improving cognitive and analytic skills, Improving College Admission Test Scores—Verbal Series uses CAI to ease the pain of preparing for the Scholastic Aptitude Test. It provides practice in choosing antonyms, in seeing the relationship among parts of a sentence, in recognizing and judging the relationship between words (analogies), in reading comprehension, in grammar and usage, and in sentence correction. Although some students often review the entire program or parts of it several times, all students admit that this CAI has helped to raise their scores on the SATs.

Still another CAI package is the Microcomputer Courseware Package. Four programs help students in writing complete sentences, expanding sentences, using outlining skills, and writing complete paragraphs. Typical of the comments from students who use these instructional aids is, "I'm beginning to understand the correct construction of a paragraph." This student used the package called Final Assembly: Writing Complete Paragraphs.

After students have completed CAI on the use of parallel structure or punctuation in a package entitled The Writing Lab, I ask them to write a paragraph (or paragraphs) on a topic of their choice to see that they have mastered, or at least have a very good understanding of, both principles. Perhaps the gorilla logo fascinates the students at first, but their willingness to continue with The Writing Lab lessons and their performance when working on their own show that they have strengthened their writing techniques, such as in sentence combining, using correct pronoun reference, and avoiding run-on sentences and misplaced modifiers.

Some discerning students recognize what their English teachers will be stressing, which prompts them to come to the lab on their own for CAI exercises. Practice with the materials helps them to understand a particular technique before it is introduced and studied in the classroom. One student came to the lab for advance help on how to recognize and use noun clauses correctly. He had employed noun clauses in his writing, but he did not understand how or why he had used them. After he completed Noun Clauses, we discussed papers in which he had used some noun clauses.

If students praise the worth of CAI, who could ask for more? Although the clinician, tutor, or director of a writing lab must still be present to encourage and assist students as they achieve mastery of writing skills, CAI helps immeasurably toward arriving at that goal.

COMPUTER SOFTWARE AT THE WRITE PLACE
Mt. Lebanon Senior High School

Bank Street Writer—Word Processor
Broderbund Software
17 Paul Drive
San Rafael, CA 94903

Complete Writer for the Bank Street Writer
Learnco Incorporated
128 High Street
Greenland, NH 03840

Apple Writer II
Apple Computer, Inc.
20525 Mariani Avenue
Cupertino, CA 95014

Link It All Together: Writing Complete Sentences
Sentence Helpers: Expanding Sentences
Final Assembly: Writing Complete Paragraphs
Essential Study Skills: Using Outlining Skills
Media Materials, Inc.
2936 Remington Avenue
Baltimore, MD 21211

Peter Funk's Wordskill
Bede Software, Inc.
Princeton, NJ 08540

Sentences and Fragments
Micro Power & Light Co.
12820 Hillcrest Road
Suite 224
Dallas, TX 75230

The Writing Lab from Gorilla Software
Simpac Educational Systems
Gainesville, FL 32602

Computer Assisted Writing
Writing Competency
Capitalization—Uses of the Capital Letter
Punctuation
Quotation Marks
Educational Activities, Inc.
Microcomputer Programs
Freeport, NY 11520

All about Commas
Microcomputer Software by Milton Bradley Co.
Education Division
443 Shaker Road
East Longmeadow, MA 01028

Logical Reasoning
Noun Clauses
Practical Composition Package
Punctuation Review
Sentences
Intellectual Software
798 North Avenue
Bridgeport, CT 06606

Improving College Admission Test Scores—Verbal Series
Analogies, Opposites, Sentence Completion
Reading Comprehension
Standard Written English
NASSP
1904 Association Drive
Reston, VA 22091

Vocabulary Adventure I
Vocabulary Adventure II: The Labyrinth
Queue
5 Chapel Hill Drive
Fairfield, CT 06432

Vocabulary Series—24 Programs
MicroEd, Inc.
P.O. Box 444005
Eden Prairie, MN 55344

Whole Brain Spelling—Main Word List
Sublogic Communications Corp.
713 Edgebrook Drive
Champaign, IL 61820

IV Wider Horizons

19 High School-College Collaboration

Henry A. Luce
Thomas G. Ferguson Associates, Inc.
Parsippany, New Jersey

In a very perceptive and realistic discussion of the future of writing centers, Jeanne Simpson explains that "the writing center movement has expanded because writing center people have learned to communicate—to form a network, to transmit information, and to exchange assistance" (Simpson 1985, 3). One especially exciting and rapidly growing area for the kind of exchange of which Simpson speaks is that of high school-college collaboration in writing centers. Moreover, those of us who have been fortunate enough to participate in such collaborations can offer one other observation: they are also a lot of fun. Those institutions who are looking to expand or improve their writing centers, indeed their entire writing programs, would do well to consider high school-college collaboration. The need is there; the time is right.

These are rough days for those of us in education, and I'm sure we have all heard the lament before: in the face of declining enrollments and rising academic underpreparedness, of retrenched faculties and budgetary constraints, of sharply shifting federal mandates and weakened public confidence, all levels of the American educational system are experiencing this national crisis. In a study of undergraduate education, Ernest L. Boyer, President of the Carnegie Foundation for the Advancement of Teaching, discovered "one of our most disturbing findings is the discontinuity that exists between the public schools and institutions of higher learning" (Boyer 1986, 284).

Part of this national crisis, but more pertinent to our purposes here, is the much discussed "writing crisis." From lengthy reports by prestigious national commissions, to hundreds of articles in local newspapers and magazines, the evidence is everywhere and overwhelming. It has become, according to Joyce Steward and Mary Croft, authors of *The Writing Laboratory*, "everywhere the loudest noise in education"

(Steward and Croft 1982, 2). Furthermore, at a time when society is becoming increasingly complex, when more and more underprepared students are being encouraged to attend college, the problem is exacerbated by the fact that many teachers are themselves underprepared in the teaching of composition. Theories of writing process approaches differ greatly from the traditional methods of teaching composition. And as Brannon and Knoblauch note, many student writers have been harmed by teachers who have "exaggerated formal and technical constraints" (Brannon and Knoblauch 1984, 43).

But if both precollege and postsecondary education are indeed in crisis, then for both the way out is clear. Collaborative efforts make the transition more successful for students. It is, clearly, in the mutual interest of both sectors to do so. Because of their concern for the "literacy crisis," the Modern Language Association has established a Commission on Writing and Literature (1983) whose charges include identifying "ways in which MLA and ADE can support the teaching of writing and literature in secondary schools" (MLA 1988, 70). In 1987, the National Writing Center Association, comprised primarily of college members, elected two high school teachers to its executive board and another the following year. They even plan to publish a position statement for high school writing centers.

A significant amount of collaboration is already under way. The Carnegie Foundation itself in 1983 published the first in a series of special reports, Gene Maeroff's *School and College: Partnerships in Education;* in 1985 as part of its series *New Directions for Teaching and Learning,* Jossey-Bass published William T. Daly's "College-School Collaboration: Appraising the Major Approaches." The Yale-New Haven Teachers Institute, one of the oldest and most successful collaborative programs, has been under way since 1978. Increasingly, federal agencies and private foundations have been funding collaborative projects. The Commission on Writing and Literature reports that "specific collaborative projects (e.g., the National Writing Project) have made significant improvements in the teaching of writing" (MLA 1988, 74). With specific regard to collaboration through writing centers, programs in one form or another have begun in California, Colorado, Florida, Illinois, Indiana, Massachusetts, Nebraska, New Jersey, New York, Ohio, Pennsylvania, South Dakota, Utah, and Wisconsin.

Different in purpose and design though they may be, writing center collaborations are beginning to flourish because, quite simply, they make sense. When an individual school tries to address its own particular writing crisis, it discovers all too frequently that it is inadequate to the task, not because it lacks the skill or commitment required, but because it lacks the larger perspective from which to examine and evaluate its programs. For example, a high school English department cannot effectively prepare its students for the demands of college writing unless it knows what colleges expect from incoming freshmen. Similarly, a college cannot very well design its program unless it knows how high schools have prepared students. Collaboration between the sectors, then, becomes the means for bridging the gap between high school and college, for ensuring the continuity of excellence throughout the system.

This is not as easily done as it might appear, however. Indeed, to some people the entire notion might seem a bit radical. American institutions of higher education have traditionally had very little to do with secondary education, especially since World War II. So if American education is to improve to the extent now demanded by public and private sectors alike, then collegiality must become the most natural act of all.

It is imperative that college instructors, too long aloof, isolated, and absorbed in the demands of their own disciplines, come to understand and appreciate the concerns and priorities of—and the demands made upon—their colleagues in the secondary schools. College instructors need to ask themselves how realistic they are in their assumptions about high school writing instruction and in their expectations about the writing performance of incoming freshmen. They need to know more about the objectives of high school writing programs, the teaching strategies, the nature of writing activities, and the evaluation practices. Such an understanding will go a long way towards enabling college instructors to deal with the often bewildering array of problems their students seem to arrive with.

Five classes, a homeroom, cafeteria duty, and assorted other obligations leave high school teachers with precious little time for scholarly activities such as research and experimentation. But they have a tremendous amount to offer to the collaborative experience. Hence, it is equally imperative that there be made available to high school teachers a mechanism that can incorporate into current pedagogical theory their experiences, insights, and approaches. That mechanism can be writing center collaboration.

Though now widely appreciated as being of tremendous value to students, writing centers as currently utilized in most schools and colleges have offered little help to the great number of teachers of composition—at any level—who are in need of improving their own teaching skills. Certainly, like writing itself, the teaching of writing can always improve. And it is here that the writing center becomes even more valuable.

A writing center collaboration can provide teachers with a splendid opportunity to interact with their colleagues and to share experiences, strategies, and insights into the teaching of writing. Such a collaboration offers teachers a freedom and flexibility unavailable in the traditional classroom situation. In the writing center, the opportunity exists to develop and refine diagnostic and conferencing skills, to experiment with new strategies and new techniques, to test the effectiveness of various materials and to develop new ones.

Thus, in addition to bridging the gap between high school and college, a writing center collaboration also bridges the gap between rhetorical theories and classroom activities. The result, beneficial to teachers and students alike, is an on-going and growing community of writers, mutually supportive, mutually instructive.

I mentioned earlier that such a collaboration has an additional benefit: it's fun. These days, not much of what we do in our profession can make that claim. In the discussion of the two very different examples that follows, I am sure that the enthusiasm, the energy, the sheer good will of the participants towards their projects will make this last point readily apparent.

Begun in 1984 and designated an NCTE Center of Excellence in 1986, the Kenmore Project is a splendid example of high school/college collaboration through writing centers.

According to Rosa Bhakuni, Director of the Kenmore High School Writing Lab, the project was initiated by Dr. Harold Foster, Associate Professor of English Education at the University of Akron. As part of the requirements for his course "Instructional Techniques in English," Dr. Foster places each of his Akron students for one hour per week with an experienced English teacher at Kenmore High School. Initial placements were made in English classrooms where the Akron students observed and wrote reaction papers about such matters as teacher technique, student motivation and behavior, and class structure. The extension of the placement to—indeed the eventual establishment of—the Kenmore Writing Lab was a happy consequence of the success of and steadily increasing enrollment in Dr. Foster's class.

Akron students who had no teacher to visit, but who were interested in doing so, were invited to tutor high school students on their writing. At first, this tutoring took place in the back of classrooms, in halls, in empty classrooms, and in the library. Eventually, through the efforts of Mr. Harry Jordan, the Kenmore principal, a room was secured and the Kenmore Writing Lab was born.

Through their work in the Kenmore lab, the University of Akron students become familiar with the process approach to teaching writing, as well as with one-to-one tutoring and conferencing techniques. Part of their final grade for Dr. Foster's course is determined by several papers written to evaluate their experiences in the writing lab. Ms. Bhakuni notes that "From this group of tutors, one or two are invited to student teach at Kenmore High. . . . and ideally, the student teacher who excels may be asked to join the faculty after graduation."

The Kenmore project is so successful because it truly is a partnership, with significant benefits for all the participants:

1. *The college students*: Because the project ensures their active participation rather than passive observation, they are better trained, more highly qualified future teachers. Furthermore, the Akron students become thoroughly familiar with the realities of teaching as a career; hence, they are better able to judge if it is the career for them.

2. *The Kenmore students*: They receive the benefits of a process-oriented, conference-centered approach to writing instruction. In addition, the element of peer collaboration helps their development as writers and adds to their confidence in its own unique ways. And all of the attention focused on them and their writing reinforces the importance of effective communication.

3. *The Kenmore faculty*: All of the participating teachers understandably appreciate the well-qualified, motivated college students who help them by grading papers, presenting units on literature, and conferencing with the high school writers. Moreover, the teachers benefit from the fact that the college students and their faculty make available the latest in composition research and theory. They are valuable sources of information concerning new strategies and techniques.

4. *The University*: Clearly, such a program benefits the University of Akron by attracting first-rate students to its education department. It provides these students with what Ms. Bhakuni calls "a needed proving ground." And, too, such community involvement makes for wonderful public relations, a benefit not to be underestimated in times of shrinking enrollment and increased competition for good students.

Although not as formally structured as the Kenmore Project—and as yet unfunded—the writing center collaboration between Red Bank Regional High School and Monmouth College, both New Jersey institutions, is a good example of what can be done with a little imagination and a great deal of enthusiasm. It also serves as an example of how years of lack of communication between the sectors can be overcome.

In the spring of 1983, representatives from Monmouth College and several area high schools met to identify common problems and, working collaboratively, to attempt to develop possible solutions. The idea and the energy behind the meeting belonged to Dr. Robert Andreach, former Associate Professor of English at the college, and at that time the Coordinator of Developmental Education. As one of the Monmouth College representatives, I submitted a proposal for a kind of writing center exchange program as one way of dealing with the writing problems we all were facing.

Essentially, what the idea called for was to bring to the college's writing center faculty from area high schools to observe the center's operation firsthand and to share with college writing instructors strategies, experiences and approaches to teaching writing. The project further called for bringing to the college's writing center potential high school peer tutors for training alongside the Monmouth peer tutors, after which they would return to staff their own centers. The directors of the centers would continue to meet regularly, sometimes with tutors, sometimes without, to share things that worked and to discard things that didn't.

The idea, though a good one, was hardly revolutionary. In fact, I later learned that the City University of New York had been involved in a similar project for several years and that another one was under way at the University of South Dakota. Still, it seemed like a pretty good idea to me, one that certainly should be pursued. It also seemed like a good idea to Pamela Farrell, English teacher and Director of the Writing Center at Red Bank Regional High School; so good in fact, that she had thought of it nearly two years earlier and had sent her proposal along to the college.

It is embarrassing but nonetheless important to note that the Department of English at Monmouth College simply ignored her proposal. Whether through arrogance or ignorance or innocence does not really matter. The point is that, in those days, collaboration between the sectors had not yet become fashionable; articulation was not yet a buzz word. And writing centers were themselves still suspect to some people. This attitude was, I suspect, typical of that at too many colleges. Unfortunately, it may still be at some.

Fortunately, also present at the initial meeting was Dr. Robert Nogueira, the principal of Red Bank Regional High School. He told Pamela Farrell about the rebirth of the idea, and she contacted me during the summer. We began to get to know each other, to discuss writers, writing, and writing centers. Very quickly it became "Pam" and "Hank." We formulated a plan we could both live with and wrote our proposal.

We encountered another significant problem. Our proposal was only one part of a six-proposal/seven-school collaborative package that, though well intentioned, was simply way too unwieldy and unfocused to be taken seriously by any funding agency, either public or private. Quite frankly, Eisenhower's plans for the invasion of Normandy were less complicated than this grant proposal. The responses from several funding agencies were the same: no money.

It was at this point that we decided to ignore bureaucracies and budgets and just try to get something going for the fall of 1984. In the interim, rather than lose touch with each other, we made a point of getting involved in each other's writing activities in any way we could. This turned out to be a wonderful idea.

Pam and I visited each other's writing centers, of course. But we did quite a few other things as well. I accepted an invitation from Pam to attend the Red Bank Regional High School Performing Arts Festival, with which Pam was deeply involved. Many of her creative writers were also prospective peer tutors. In turn, Pam brought some of her creative writing students to a Monmouth College English Department-sponsored reading of works of original fiction by college faculty. We met each other's supervisors and administrators; our students got used to seeing us together. All of this interaction and emphasis on writing, including nonacademic kinds of writing, made collaboration a reality even before we started our tutor training program. When the time did come to start, we knew exactly what we wanted to do and we trusted each other to be able to do it.

Our goal this time was modest, yet it was one that would greatly enrich and improve both of our writing centers. We set out to establish a community of writers, and we wanted our tutors to see their writing centers in just this way. Thus, each center—admittedly serving different populations and with different circumstances and needs—was to be a place where students could come and do some writing, could learn about writing, and perhaps most important of all could talk about their own writing problems and experiences with an interested, well-trained reader/listener. That reader/listener is the tutor, and learning how and when and what to respond to is what our tutor training program would be all about.

The plan was similar to the original: bring the Red Bank Regional tutors to the college's writing center to train along with the Monmouth College writing tutors. This training would entail writing, role-playing, listening, questioning, observing, information-sharing. Tutors would sit-in on and then participate in actual tutoring sessions being conducted by experienced Monmouth College tutors. Then we would talk some more. Interested faculty from both schools were invited to participate, and through Pam's good offices we were able to have Dr. Nancy Sommers from Rutgers University (now of Harvard University) conduct a final workshop for us on responding to student writing.

During the course of the training, Pam and I were purposefully obvious in our sharing of the workload, the responsibility, and the expertise. We kept saying that collaborative learning was what a writing center was all about. And we felt strongly that if the collaboration between the schools was to work in the way we believed it could, we had to demonstrate it ourselves as well as talk about it.

We were delighted with the way things worked out. Perhaps more important, so were the tutors. They were exposed to a huge amount of information in a short period, and, in fact, had to rethink many of their old views of writing and writing instruction. But they found, too, that the program gave them increased confidence, made them feel quite professional, and was thoroughly enjoyable to boot. Taking their cue from Pam and me, both high school tutors and college tutors found the collaboration to be the most natural thing in the world. They encouraged us to do it again the following year.

Year two of our collaborative project saw a second high school join us. Having heard favorably of the arrangement, Monmouth Regional High School from Tinton Falls, New Jersey, asked to participate and has since become a regular participant. Initially needing assistance in setting up its own writing center, Monmouth Regional is now a full-fledged contributing partner.

To celebrate our third year of collaboration, we decided to go for broke and conclude our four days of tutor training and information sharing with a day-long, statewide conference entitled "Collaboration: Thinking, Writing, Reading." Sponsored by Red Bank Regional High School in cooperation with Monmouth College and the New Jersey Council of Teachers of English, the conference brought to the Monmouth campus over two hundred faculty and administrators from schools and colleges across the state.

David Bartholomae of the University of Pittsburgh and Art Young of Michigan Technological University (now of Clemson University) were the featured speakers. Concurrent workshops led by high school and college experts followed each speaker and addressed such topics as using the humanities as a catalyst for thinking, writing, and reading; teaching Shakespeare to basic readers; and student literacy and the media. The conference also included a book exhibit by Boynton/Cook Publishers and a poetry reading featuring two award-winning New Jersey poets, provided by the Geraldine R. Dodge Foundation.

I would like to say that the reason the conference was such a smashing success (and it was) was that Pam and I are such professionals and so expert at such things. We do make a good team, I admit. But the real reason our conference received such a tremendous response and such good reviews was that the need was there, and the time was right. This was the theme we heard time and again both during the conference and in the correspondence we received following it. We were asked to please do it again next year, and I suspect we shall. More important, and ultimately perhaps more lasting, would be for other schools and colleges to begin collaborations of their own. These need not be elaborate, expensive, multi-school arrangements. Simply visiting the writing center of a nearby school or college is enough to start. From there the only limits are energy and imagination.

References

Boyer, Ernest L., "Smoothing the Transition from School to College." *Phi Delta Kappan* 68 (December 1986).

Brannon, Lil, and C. H. Knoblauch. "A Philosophical Perspective on Writing Centers and the Teaching of Writing." In *Writing Centers: Theory and Administration,* edited by Gary A. Olson. Urbana, Ill.: NCTE, 1984.

Modern Language Association. "Report of the Commission on Writing and Literature." In *Profession 88.* New York: MLA, 1988.

Simpson, Jeanne. "What Lies Ahead for Writing Centers: A Position Statement on Professional Concerns." *The Writing Center Journal* 6 (1985).

Joyce S. Steward and Mary K. Croft. *The Writing Laboratory: Organization, Management and Methods.* Glenview, Ill.: Scott, Foresman and Co., 1982.

20 Writing Across the Curriculum

Barbara Brooks
Pattonville High School
Maryland Heights, Missouri

Introduction

The Pattonville Senior High School Writing Center is staffed with writing coaches from our English Department. We are open six hours a day with one writing coach each hour. Located in the English wing, the room is equipped with 19 Apple IIe computers and five printers. We have an enclosed entrance way where one-on-one conferencing can be conducted while word-processing activities can continue in the main room (see figure 3 in chapter 4).

The writing center always begins its year with a gala open house party. We allow two to three weeks at the beginning of the year to set up the writing center and to have our coaches practice our most frequently used programs. It is very important that we work as a team rather than as four individuals assigned to a particular hour in the center. Each needs to know what the other is doing if we are to be effective. Our first team effort is the open house. We design and distribute posters, announcements, and invitations. All faculty members and staff can stop by during their planning period since the event occurs for the entire day. Many colleagues use this opportunity to book a presentation or to discuss their writing needs with us. Often we are lesson designers as well as presenters, and faculty have come to expect handouts along with their presentations.

Classroom Presentations

Our most popular presentations involve teaching research skills, demonstrating how to answer essay questions, and explaining how to write book reports for nonfiction as well as fiction books. We always work in conjunction with the requesting faculty member in preparing the presentation. For example, a chemistry teacher offers a research paper as extra credit but asks the writing center to give a one-hour presentation on everything from how to write a thesis statement to how to handle research material complete with footnotes and bibliography. First, we find out the basic facts, such as the grade level of the students, the size of the class, and the hours needed. Then we ask for sample papers (if available), the textbook, and a list of possible sources the students would be expected to use. The particular needs of this teacher focus on writing a decent thesis statement that lends itself to research and critical thinking rather than an informational report. The teacher also wants students to follow APA guidelines. Our job is to help this teacher's students meet the requirements of the assignment.

We begin the presentation by defining a thesis statement and then by showing students how to take a topic and narrow it down to a statement of purpose. We stress that the research provides the information and that the students provide the analysis of it. With the use of an overhead projector, we explain how to create a working bibliography and how to take notes by either quoting, outlining, or paraphrasing. We then discuss how to properly introduce the research material and correctly use footnotes. A prepared handout shows the standard forms for footnotes and bibliography according to APA guidelines. The handout also includes hints on the organization of the paper: introduction with thesis statement last; at least three body paragraphs; and a conclusion that either summarizes or extrapolates. Finally, we remind students that the writing center is open all day and that they should sign up for an appointment if they would like further help or clarification.

We give a similar presentation to the sophomore world history classes with an emphasis on comparisons. Research, footnotes, and bibliography are also required, but we spend considerable time explaining the organization of a comparison paper. These students are also encouraged to learn how to word process, so their teacher has all of them come to the writing center to type in their introductory paragraphs. The majority of the students return for follow-up visits to finish processing their papers and to get help along the way with development.

Other Services

Another service we offer to our colleagues is one-on-one tutoring of software programs. Teachers can come to the writing center during their planning hour and learn Apple Writer. They have found this especially helpful in writing tests and then saving them on disk and being able to easily make changes from semester to semester. Another time-saver program that is popular with our teachers is Crossword Magic and Word Search. No more figuring out where to place words on the grid; it is all done by computer. Probably the most revered piece of software we have is a grade book program called Flash Grader that was especially designed by a district patron. We can instruct our teachers in this program in about fifteen minutes and it truly saves them hours of time. Our most recent acquisition is the Test Writer program, a product of Coronado Publishers. It allows for random selection of test items and merging of files for truly teacher-made tests. Another favorite continues to be Print Shop, with its endless possibilities for banners and signs. We teach most of these programs individually, but we also hold mini-workshops after school for small groups of teachers.

Successful WAC Projects

Economics—Problem Solving

This presentation moves the students from topic selection to thesis statement by brainstorming and clustering together. We proceed to formulate a possible outline for a proposed topic. We solicit facts and examples as the best means of development and demonstrate an organizational pattern. We include a few pointers about how to handle the research material and offer a list of transition words to aid in the writing process.

Social Studies—Philosophy Paper

Students enhance their study of history by doing research on great philosophers and then defining their own philosophy of life in terms of what they have learned. For this sophomore class we designed a worksheet with specific areas of focus that the students could use while doing their research. We made a return visit after library time was finished to demonstrate how to organize their notes into a piece of writing.

Home Economics—Nonfiction Book Report

The needs of the Home Economics department centered around getting the students to write a successful report on the nonfiction books they were reading. We first prepared a handout of standard information to include in book reports, and then we used the overhead projector and a student's rough draft to show how to write the report. We emphasized making subjective connections from objective statements.

Journalism—Newsroom

Our journalism classes learn how to use the Newsroom software package and are thereby able to print a one- to two-page weekly paper in addition to the monthly "slick" paper. Also, our students have learned a program designed especially for yearbooks and are producing the entire yearbook with the aid of computers. Naturally, this kind of commitment ties up our computers. For the Newsroom program, the students are allotted three hours per week and sometimes have to sign up for extra time the same way other students do. With the yearbook program, we have to set up double disk drives and generally, when the students' deadlines approach their teacher makes provision to use the writing center after school hours.

Freshman English—Writing Process

We have made word processing a goal for all of our freshmen. After students become familiar with the writing process and peer editing, they are signed up as a class for writing center time. Here, they type in their rough drafts and receive a printout for editing. After two students edit their writing, they return to make revisions. Their final drafts are often made into class booklets of which each student receives a copy.

Science—Saturation Paper

The annual field trip to the zoo has turned into a profitable lesson on writing a saturation paper. At the request of a science teacher, we designed an observation sheet asking for specific information about the various places visited in the zoo. We then gave a classroom presentation on note taking and, with the use of the overhead projector, demonstrated how to find a focus and organize the notes into a report.

The success of the writing center has enhanced our reputation across departments, throughout the school. As teachers become satisfied with our presentations and see how their students' work improves, they become our most enthusiastic supporters. Their conviction that we are a vital and necessary service to our school has accounted for much of our growth. Students do not hesitate to come to the writing center for help with any type of writing problem from any class. We frequently get requests for help with extra credit reports from disciplines that do very little formal writing. Teachers encourage students to use the center by allowing them to visit during class time, but many of our students come to the writing center from study hall. Regardless of why they come to see us, we are happy we can be of service to our faculty and our students.

21 Community Connections

Rosa I. Bhakuni
University of Akron and
Kenmore High School Writing Lab

The first time Marie came to the writing lab, she walked cautiously and slowly, clutching her purse and notebook to her chest. In a thin voice, she told the tutor, "The teacher sent me here to write."

The tutor asked, "What about?"

Marie said, "I don't know."

"Did you read the assignment?" the tutor probed.

"No," said Marie, looking worried.

"Well, then, I suggest you go back to class, read the assignment, and come back tomorrow prepared to write. I'll write a note to your teacher and issue you a pass, so you won't get in trouble."

That afternoon, the tutor inquired about the student to the teacher. Marie had been out of school for six months while she carried and delivered a baby. That day was her first back to school, and she was thoroughly confused about the work to be done. The next day, the tutor attempted to set Marie at ease and probed for a topic that interested the student: the new baby.

Marie attended the writing lab for five consecutive days, handing in her first written assignment of the year. On her last visit to the lab, as she glanced at her final draft of five days' work, she smiled to the tutor saying, "And I was so scared to write! Writing isn't that hard."

The anecdote about Marie serves to show that, at times, the writing lab, with its one-to-one tutoring, becomes a "halfway house" for students who have been absent from school for a long time. Perhaps Marie could have eventually caught up with her peers in class, but the writing lab gave her the individual help she needed to bridge the gap of the six-month absence. Moreover, the writing lab tutor, with patience, understanding, and knowledge of the writing process, guided her through the steps in writing, allowing Marie to become confident as a writer.

Developing confidence in student writers, providing a nonthreatening atmosphere in a writing place, and supporting the student in experimenting with the written word are part of what a writing lab offers. Tutors and lab directors who possess vision can extend the use of the writing lab to provide help not only for students and teachers, but also to the community. These ties to the community start once school opens in September. During the first open house, the writing lab is open and demonstrating its services. Tutors present a sample of a tutoring conference to visitors, so they can watch what goes on at the lab. The lab is also open during the parent-teacher conferences. As a matter of course, directors ask teachers to mention the writing lab and its merits to visiting parents who are interested in the scholastic welfare of their children. Shortly before these events, the director writes a short article for the local newspaper, school newspaper, local radio or television news. With proper planning, tutors get interviewed by a local television station or newspaper, thus educating the community about the free resources provided for their children by the school. Groups such as the PTA have also visited our lab, and after asking questions about its program, often mention to their children that they should attend. Parents' support strengthens the work of the writing lab.

To reach the local Board of Education, the Kenmore High School Writing Lab allowed the school system's communications crew to come into the lab and film students and tutors at work. They filmed students writing, collaborating, reading their papers aloud to each other; they interviewed the director; and they caught a tutoring session. This film was then shown to the local Board of Education at their next meeting. The disruption caused by the film crew that day was well worth it. Although not much tutoring got done, the Akron Board of Education proposed that each high school in the system have a writing lab within the next two years.

As the writing lab opens the door to students, teachers, and the whole school, it can also build bridges to the community. As spokespeople for the writing lab, tutors and directors speak to public groups such as Kiwanis, Lions Clubs, and Junior League about the advantages of the writing lab. There have been times when a professional in one of these groups offers support to the lab for a needed item that is unaffordable within the lab budget. Local companies in the computer field lend computers and software for students to try out.

Many community service groups sponsor annual writing contests, and they can use the writing lab as a center to distribute essays and use tutors as judges for these contests. This fall, the writing lab is helping students to write for the United Fund Contest and is urging Kenmore High School students to compete in the Lucille Loy Kuck Ohioana Award for Excellence in Creative Writing, as well as other scholarship-winning writing awards. Moreover, winning entries are posted at the lab, where they are read by the winners to invited guests from the school and community. The writing lab, as the center of writing in a school, is the place to post information about writing contests and to sponsor and encourage those writing contests within the school and the community. The final touch is for the lab to also take part in encouraging writing by establishing prizes and creating writing contests that are open to students in the school. After the winners are chosen, the lab publishes their work through the local newspaper.

Students have seldom seen their writing in print. The writing lab photocopies prize-winning essays in booklet form to encourage winners to keep writing. Another tie between the writing lab and the community is to invite local professional writers to an afternoon of readings by the students, to answer questions about writing posed by interested students, or perhaps to critique some of the student writers' work.

There is a wealth of information in the writing lab, once it opens its doors to students, teachers, the school, and the community. There is also a wealth of information that can be tapped for research. Since the lab encourages experimentation with the written word, it is the obvious place to do research. School teachers learning about the writing process can tap that lode from as close as the school where they teach. Tutors, who are often college students or graduate students, can find the writing lab the topic needed for a research paper, an observation, ethnographic research, or a dissertation problem. The writing lab becomes then a resource to college students and universities. A writing lab director who keeps abreast of the latest published literature about writing labs can research a particular style of tutoring or a solution to a problem in writing; staff can gather information to present in a paper at one of the writing lab conferences held annually.

Writing no longer has to be an isolated activity. Writing is communication and collaboration. The writing lab, working along with the community, allows the students to participate in creating ties with the real world around them.

22 Community and the Writing Lab

John Neil Graham
Valentine Middle School
Valentine, Nebraska

At the Valentine Middle School, all of the seventh- and eighth-grade students come to the writing lab each day because it is a required class. The writing lab has replaced a morning study hall. Now the students alternate every twelve weeks between writing lab, art, and physical education. The assignments consist of individual daily writing assignments and individual and group writing projects. Most of the students' assignments take them into the community for research, sharing, and publication.

The autobiography assignment requires the students to write about their past, present, and future. This task sends them into the community to do research into their own family's background, since a majority of the students' families still reside locally. The assignment also allows the students to look ahead to what the community will offer them in regard to school and job possibilities.

The middle school students share their writings with the community in various ways. They write a weekly poetry section for the local paper that is based on poems or freewriting taken from their personal writing folders. The students write and record radio spots for National Education Week: these are ten-, twenty-, and thirty-second announcements concerning the students' feelings toward education. The students also write Christmas cards to armed services personnel who are stationed overseas during the holidays.

I teach a weekly expressive writing class at Pine View Good Samaritan Center; the middle school students also share their work with the residents of this facility. For example, one of the middle school students' assignments is to write about old age or the aging process. I take those writings and let the residents expand them. One student wrote the following:

147

The Old Fashion Days

A girl in her long dress and bonnet,
With new bright designs on it.
A man in his black hat,
Wearing it wherever he is at.
They were simple in their ways,
In those long ago old fashion days.

A one-room cabin was their house,
In the evening it was quiet as a mouse.
Someone would tell a riddle,
While another would play a fiddle.
They were simple in their ways,
In those long ago old fashion days.

The residents took the idea and the form and produced this poem:

The Old Fashion Days

A girl in her long dress and bonnet,
With new bright designs on it.
A man in his black hat,
Wearing it wherever he is at.
They were simple in their ways,
In those long ago old fashion days.

A one-room log cabin was their house,
In the evening it was quiet as a mouse.
A heated brick with protective wrapping,
Kept them warm until the rooster's flapping.
They were simple in their ways,
In those long ago old fashion days.

The Saturday night bath in the old wash tub,
Was a place you could sit and scrub.
In the summer it was fun,
But in the winter it was pick up your towel and run.
They were simple in their ways,
In those long ago old fashion days.

Lumber wagons supplied,
The things upon which they relied.
Gardens were planted and raised,
And the good Lord was always praised.
They were tough in their ways,
In those long ago old fashion days.

The cook toted a gun and a Climax chew,
While he concocted his ole stew.
The ingredients were never the same,
But rabbits and prairie chickens were always the game.
They were tough in their ways,
In those long ago old fashion days.

Cream and butter were stored in the well,
You had to keep it sweet or the baby would yell.
Hams were smoked or put in brine,
Salty enough to float an egg just fine.
They were tough in their ways,
In those long ago old fashion days.

By Amy Hartgrave and The Pine View Residents
(Used with permission.)

On another assignment, I asked the students at each site to write an "I Wish" poem. The middle school students were astonished as I read the residents' poems to them. The middle school students had written about obtaining cars, houses, money, and other material possessions, while the residents wrote about the pain of growing old and dying.

I Wish

I wish I would be in my own home.
I wish I could see better.
I wish I could hear better.
I wish God would take me in my sleep.
I wish it didn't cost so much here.
I wish the doctors didn't give me so many pills.

By Ella Reddick
(Used with permission.)

The students' and residents' individual and group writings are published in *The Heart City Writing Shop*. I type the poems the students and I have selected, and then we use the school's copier to print the sheets. This publication is printed once every twelve weeks for each section of the middle school that uses the writing lab. Each student and resident receives a copy, and copies are circulated throughout the community and sent to the directors of the Nebraska Writing Project.

Some students and residents have had their work published in other releases. A local printing company asked the writing lab students to write Valentine's Day poems, and the company chose one middle school student's poem for publication. One thousand copies have been printed this year, and another thousand will be printed next year. Also, the residents submitted several of their writings to The Nebraska Writing and Storytelling Festival. Four residents had their writings published in the Festival's booklet.

Word has spread that the writing lab needs to be used. Several teachers have given us ideas for writing projects, along with members of the community. As the students write, they are very careful with their content and grammar because they know their audience is not only fellow students and their teachers, but also a whole community

who might read their material. Feedback for writing lab students is
also very important, and the students and residents do receive tremendous response. Relatives and friends call the students and residents
when their work appears in the paper. Several students have received
letters from the service personnel to whom they have written. By
using the community as an audience for the writing lab, a powerful
interaction takes place between the writers and their audience.

Appendix A
True Confessions of High School
Writing Center Directors

The following pages speak for themselves. Each director responds honestly from personal experience. I have included only some of the answers to my interview questions in order to avoid redundancy. Although the author of each response remains anonymous, I give credit to the following directors for their candid answers and suggested readings: Elizabeth Ackley, Indian Hills High School; Rosa Bhakuni, Kenmore High School; Barbara Brooks, Pattonville High School; Carol Lefelt, Highland Park High School; Amy Levin, Scarsdale High School; Betty Barbara Sipe, Mt. Lebanon High School; Sharon Sorenson, Central High School; Pat Stoddart, Logan High School; Jim Upton, Burlington Community High School; Leslie Wilson, Homewood-Flossmoor High School; and Kim Zupec, Warren Township High School.

What was the hardest part of getting your writing lab/center started?

Convincing the appropriate people, the superintendent and the school board, of the need for a writing lab. In addition, funding for equipping a writing lab and for the salary of an additional staff member proved essential.

Convincing the high school faculty and staff that the writing lab is a worthwhile project needing their support, and that it would not threaten their teaching techniques nor their approach to writing.

Getting administrators and other staff members to understand the concept and logistics of how it could work.

What was the easiest part?

Getting the kids into the lab. After a bit of coaxing, we have recruited many faithful attendees.

Working with the tutors themselves—they understand the non-directive approach.

Witnessing the student tutor-to-tutee relationship; the one-to-one rapport was almost automatic.

151

Did you have any unusual experiences?

I was surprised at the politics involved in starting a new project within a school system. Benefiting students is not the principal category by which projects get funded and supported. I was also surprised that teachers were threatened by the establishment of a writing lab. Many thought it would bring more work for them and that staff in the writing lab would judge their performance teaching writing, their writing assignments, and their knowledge of the latest theories of composition.

What would you recommend to new directors? Please include any physical, mental, emotional, inspirational recommendations.

A paragraph is too small to make these kinds of recommendations. The hurdles are unbelievable—jealousy from those who didn't come up with the idea, cynicism from those who never want to try anything new, frustration from those who are eager to use the facilities but find scheduling impossible, exhaustion on the part of the person responsible for working with several hundred students per week and maintaining the records to provide continuity, antagonism from administrators who don't want to be bothered with scheduling. Rewards? Only from the dozens of students whose eyes light up with understanding.

Physical stamina—when working in the lab, the teacher must be mobile. Mentally alert—each student has a different need, at times a different assignment, so you must be able to think of new ideas quickly. Willingness to fight for the lab—always to be ready to try new advertisement for the lab. Realize there will be criticism of the lab— be ready to shoulder that criticism. Always keep in mind this is a worthwhile and fundamental service for the student. Be willing to try new ideas—absorb the needs of the students.

In addition to the readings, attend the NWCA workshops, visit as many centers as possible, be sure to design a center to meet the needs of your particular institution, constantly evaluate and assess goals of the center. Cultivate the friendship of at least one other person who is as interested in the center as you are; you will need someone to share frustrations, failures and successes. You *must* maintain patience and a sense of humor. Maintain a journal about writing lab professional and personal experiences; it is good therapy and a needed reference for future use.

What makes the first year different from the second?

You don't have any mistakes to correct, you don't really know *how* the center will work, you are setting precedents in policy, you're *proving* the concept.

Procedures have to be developed, monitored, and revised. You have to develop a core of interested students and teachers. You have to set up channels of communication among teachers, counselors, students, tutors, and others.

Do you have any practical advice?

Keep individual and collective records. Public relations is very important!

Always focus on the positive gains students make. Send thank you notes to faculty who have requested presentations and to faculty who allow students to come to the writing center during their class time. Don't let the centers become a hangout for students who just want to miss another class.

If one is not fully committed to the concept of the center and is not willing to endure all of the hassles involved in developing one, do not attempt to do so. Also, do not believe that failures and successes are your personal responsibility.

How did you get other staff across the curriculum and the English department involved?

This is our biggest ongoing problem—we have a core of supportive teachers trained in writing across the curriculum, but others are still indifferent, skeptical, or even hostile. Our approaches included: my talking at faculty meetings and meeting with teachers during free periods; chats in faculty rooms; flyers in faculty mailboxes; posters around the school; items in newsletters; surveys; memos to teachers notifying them that their student has visited the writing center.

I volunteered to make presentations about the writing lab in class-rooms. Once I visited classrooms, I volunteered to present topics such as: term papers, the new MLA documentation, and so on. Also, when we were getting very few students to tutor, I volunteered to "look over" (read "grade") student essays for teachers. This way, I could suggest that the weak writers should be urged to attend the writing lab.

How did you get students involved as tutors and clientele?

Allow students to come during another class period. Get a teacher to bring his/her whole class in to demonstrate writing as a process (about four days). Many students return on their own with other assignments. Allow extension on papers if students make and keep a certain number of appointments.

Hand-picked tutors from my own classes and the classes of two colleagues who knew the kinds of students I needed. The first week of school, tutors went to every English class and role-played situations and advertised the center. We have posters, announcements. Some teachers encouraged their students to go.

Tutors: I contacted students who were recommended by teachers. A few also asked to participate. Students are not, however, guaranteed a half credit and the opportunity to tutor. Instead, they must participate in training, and then selections are made.

Clientele: We made flyers for distribution in English classes. I spoke in some classes, freshmen seminars, and department meetings and arranged for publicity in the bulletin, the school newspaper, and the parent newsletter. Finally, I put out flyers on parents' night and asked counselors to distribute more in their meetings with parents. The tutors made posters.

How do you keep your lab/center going?

Pacify the librarians; snoop around to make sure the tutor is there—the one law which is always fulfilled is: *You can be sure a student will appear for tutoring if the tutor is not there*—keep the halls covered with posters; keep on the lookout for opportunities to say to teachers, "Oh, why not send your students to the writing center with that assignment?"; send my own students frequently.

Hard work, determination, enthusiasm, good public relations, and support from supervising principal and department chair.

What have been your biggest problems?

Too many responsibilities assigned to me as director because, "after all, she doesn't have regular classes assigned to her; she has the time."

Failure to have the center formally established. Indifference and resistance from staff members. Frustration at limited scope of operation of the center. Frustration at unwillingness of staff members to explore uses of the center.

Convincing reluctant members of the English department to use the facility. Convincing people that this facility is not only for the basic student. Fighting to maintain the original focus and purpose of the lab from changes administrators try to institute to meet outside requirements.

If you had little or no money, what equipment and supplies would you consider bare necessities? Why? Please list in order of importance.

To get a writing lab started, you need only the following: an administrator who is always supportive and offers his/her erudite suggestions and help, and gives a lot of encouragement; a tutor or clinician who wants to help nurture in students an interest in writing by helping them to help themselves in the writing process; a non-threatening atmosphere; and one student who needs help to remediate a writing problem, to reinforce a strength, or to gain enrichment. Nothing more is needed.

An area designated as "The Writing Center" so students will always know where they can come for help. Tables and chairs so tutor and tutee can isolate themselves from the rest of the room. Some handbooks of usage and *The Bad Speller's Dictionary.*

A quiet place, tables and chairs, dictionary, paper and pencils, adequate lighting, file cabinet, and reference sources.

If you had all the money you could possibly want, what equipment and supplies would you purchase? Why? Please list in order of priorities.

A receptionist, computers and printers, telephone, Xerox machine, library of computer software, reference books for center personnel and reference books for students, time for visits to and sharings with those who have successful centers in operation, more release time to work on the center and writing activities, money for inservice programs on writing techniques for all departments, nice furniture, carpet, airconditioning.

I believe I would purchase a quality networking system, for I believe that with students being able to communicate with their peers in other localities, they would realize the importance of communicating clearly, specifically, effectively, and logically, and networking would add another cultural dimension to their young lives because they would meet and learn about demographics and living styles in our own United States.

I would also purchase a computer that permits a person to talk to the machine and see his words appear on a screen. Something tells me that this computer will do much toward improving speech communication in the future. It will improve not only oral but also written communication.

Appendix B
Suggested Reading for
Writing Center Directors

Arkin, Marian, and Barbara Shollar. *The Tutor Book*. New York: Longman, 1982.

Beck, Paula, Thom Hawkins, and Marcia Silver. "Training and Using Peer Tutors." *College English* 40 (1978): 432–49.

Brannon, Lil. "On Becoming a More Effective Tutor." In *Tutoring Writing: A Sourcebook for Writing Labs*, edited by Muriel Harris, 105–110. Glenview, Ill.: Scott, Foresman & Co., 1982.

Bruffee, Kenneth A. "The Brooklyn Plan: Attaining Intellectual Growth Through Peer-Group Tutoring." *Liberal Education* 64 (1978): 447–68.

———. "Collaborative Learning and 'The Conversation of Mankind.' " *College English* 46 (1984): 635–52.

———. "Collaborative Learning: Some Practice Models." *College English* 34 (1973): 634–43.

———. "Two Related Issues in Peer Tutoring: Program Structure and Tutor Training." *College Composition and Communication* 31 (1980): 76–79.

Budz, Judith, and Terry Grabar. "Tutorial Versus Classroom in Freshman English." *College English* 37 (1976): 654–56.

Clark, Beverly Lyon. *Talking about Writing*. Ann Arbor: University of Michigan Press, 1985.

Clark, Cheryl, and Phyllis A. Sherwood. "A Tutoring Dialogue: From Workshop to Session." *The Writing Center Journal* 1 (1981): 26–32.

Collins, James L., and Elizabeth A. Sommers, eds. *Writing-on-Line: Using Computers in the Teaching of Writing*. Upper Montclair, N.J.: Boynton/Cook, 1985.

Dawe, Charles W., and Edward A. Dornan. *One-to-One: Resources for Conference-Centered Writing*. Boston: Little, Brown, 1981.

Donovan, Timothy R., and Ben W. McClelland, eds. *Eight Approaches to Teaching Composition*. Urbana, Ill.: NCTE, 1980.

Duke, Charles. "The Student-Centered Conference and the Writing Process." *English Journal* 64 (1975): 44–47.

Elbow, Peter. *Writing with Power*. New York: Oxford University Press, 1981.

———. *Writing Without Teachers*. New York: Oxford University Press, 1973.

157

Fishman, Judith. "On Tutors, The Writing Lab, and Writing." In *Tutoring Writing: A Sourcebook for Writing Labs,* edited by Muriel Harris, 86–93. Glenview, Ill.: Scott, Foresman & Co., 1982.

———. "The Tutor as Messenger." *The Writing Center Journal* 1 (1981): 7–11.

Fraser, Scott C., et al. "Two, Three, or Four Heads Are Better Than One: Modification of College Performance by Peer Monitoring." *Journal of Educational Psychology* 69 (1977): 101–08.

Freedman, S. W., and Ellen Nold. "On Budz and Grabar's Tutorial Vs. Classroom Study." *College English* 38 (1976): 427–29.

Garrett, Marvin P. "Toward a Delicate Balance: The Importance of Role-Playing and Peer Criticism in Peer-Tutor Training." In *Tutoring Writing: A Sourcebook for Writing Labs,* edited by Muriel Harris, 94–99. Glenview, Ill.: Scott, Foresman & Co., 1982.

Garrison, Roger. *One-to-One: Making Writing Instruction Effective.* New York: Harper and Row, 1981.

Gebhart, Richard. "Teamwork and Feedback: Broadening the Base of Collaborative Writing." *College English* 42 (1980): 69–74.

Glassman, Susan. "Tutor Training on a Shoestring." In *Tutoring Writing: A Sourcebook for Writing Labs,* edited by Muriel Harris, 123–29. Glenview, Ill.: Scott, Foresman & Co., 1982.

Haring-Smith, Tori, et al. *A Guide to Writing Programs.* Glenview, Ill.: Scott, Foresman & Co., 1984.

Harris, Muriel. "Growing Pains: The Coming of Age of Writing Centers." *The Writing Center Journal* 2 (1982): 1–8.

———. *Teaching One-to-One: The Writing Conference.* Urbana, Ill.: NCTE, 1986.

———. *Tutoring Writing: A Sourcebook for Writing Labs.* Glenview, Ill.: Scott, Foresman & Co., 1982.

Hawkins, Thom. "Intimacy and Audience: The Relationship between Revision and the Social Dimension of Peer Tutoring." *College English* 42 (1980): 64–68.

Haywood, Malcolm. "Assessing Attitudes towards the Writing Center." *The Writing Center Journal* 3 (1983): 1–11.

Kail, Harvey. "Collaborative Learning in Context: The Problem with Peer Tutoring." *College English* 45 (1983): 594–99.

Kelly, Lou. "One on One, Iowa City Style: Fifty Years of Individualized Instruction in Writing." *The Writing Center Journal* 1 (1980): 4–19.

Lapidus-Saltz, Wendy. "The Effective Feedback Script: A Peer Response Procedure." *The Writing Instructor* 1 (1981): 19–25.

Laque, Carol Feiser, and Phyllis A. Sherwood. *A Laboratory Approach to Writing.* Urbana, Ill.: NCTE, 1977.

Luban, Nina, Ann Matsuhashi, and Tom Reigstad. "One-to-One to Write: Establishing an Individual-Conference Writing Place." *English Journal* 67 (1978): 30–35.

Macrorie, Ken. *Telling Writing.* Upper Montclair, N.J.: Boynton/Cook, 1985.

———. *Writing to be Read.* Upper Montclair, N.J.: Boynton/Cook, 1984.

Martin, Frances. "Close Encounters of an Ancient Kind: Readings on the Tutorial Classroom and the Writing Conference." *The Writing Center Journal* 2 (1982): 7–17.

Murray, Donald. *Learning By Teaching*. Upper Montclair, N.J.: Boynton/Cook, 1982.

———. "The Listening Eye: Reflections on the Writing Conference." *College English* 41 (1979): 13–18.

———. *Read to Write*. New York: Holt, Rinehart, Winston, 1986.

———. *Write to Learn*. New York: Holt, Rinehart, Winston, 1984.

———. *A Writer Teaches Writing*. New York: Houghton Mifflin, 1984.

North, Stephen M. "The Idea of a Writing Center." *College English* 46 (1984): 433–36.

———. "Training Tutors to Talk about Writing." *College Composition and Communication* 33 (1982): 434–41.

———. "Writing Center Diagnosis: The Composing Profile." In *Tutoring Writing: A Sourcebook for Writing Labs*, edited by Muriel Harris, 45–52. Glenview, Ill.: Scott, Foresman & Co., 1982.

Olson, Gary A., ed. *Writing Centers: Theory and Administration*. Urbana, Ill.: NCTE, 1984.

Provost, Gary. *Make Every Word Count*. New York: Writers Digest, 1980.

Registad, Thomas J., and Donald A. McAndrew. *Training Tutors for Writing Conferences*. Urbana, Ill.: NCTE, 1984.

Roderick, John. "Problems in Tutoring." In *Tutoring Writing: A Sourcebook for Writing Labs*, edited by Muriel Harris, 32–39. Glenview, Ill.: Scott, Foresman & Co., 1982.

Sherwood, Phyllis. "What Should Tutors Know?" In *Tutoring Writing: A Sourcebook for Writing Labs*, edited by Muriel Harris, 101–104. Glenview, Ill.: Scott, Foresman & Co., 1982.

Steward, Joyce S., and Mary K. Croft. *The Writing Laboratory: Organization, Management, and Methods*. Glenview, Ill.: Scott, Foresman & Co., 1982.

Waldschmidt, Elmer C. "Peer Paired for Talk-Writing." *Illinois English Bulletin* 62 (1975): 2–8.

Weiner, Harvey. *The Writing Room*. New York: Macmillan, 1980.

Wresch, William, ed. *The Computer in Composition*. Urbana, Ill.: NCTE, 1984.

Young, Arthur, and Toby Fulwiler, eds. *Writing Across the Disciplines*. Upper Montclair, N.J.: Boynton/Cook, 1986.

All respondents suggested subscriptions to *Writing Lab Newsletter, Writing Center Journal,* and *English Journal.* They also encouraged directors to become involved in the National Writing Center Association and regional affiliates.

Appendix C
High School Writing
Center Directory

The directory includes material gathered from the survey I conducted in the spring of 1986 that may be used to create a network for high school writing center directors. It may also act as a support system for establishing, maintaining, and improving high school writing centers. The directory reflects a sampling of centers that responded to the original survey.

State: California
Name of School: Mt. Carmel High School
Address: 9550 Carmel Mountain Road
　　　　　San Diego, CA 92129
Name of Writing Lab/Center: English Computer Writing Lab
Contact Person: Betty Leal
Computers: 16 Apple IIe's
Staff: 2 English Teachers

State: California
Name of School: Vintage High School
Address: 1375 Trown Avenue
　　　　　Napa, CA 94558
Name of Writing Lab/Center: Writing Workshop
Contact Person: D. R. Wolten
Computers: None
Staff: 1 Teacher

State: Colorado
Name of School: Fort Collins High School
Address: 1400 Remington Street
　　　　　Fort Collins, CO 80524
Name of Writing Lab/Center: Computer Learning Center
Contact Person: Teresa Davies
Computers: 23 Apple IIe's
Staff: Faculty and Students

State: Florida
Name of School: Deerfield Beach High School
Address: 910 S.W. 15th Street
           Deerfield Beach, FL 33000
Name of Writing Lab/Center: Writers Workbench
Contact Person: B. Perry
Computers: 7 Apples, 15 AT&Ts
Staff: Teaching Staff

State: Illinois
Name of School: Deerfield High School
Address: 1959 Waukegan Road
           Deerfield, IL 60015
Contact Person: Kay Severns and Penny Frankel

State: Illinois
Name of School: Griffin High School
Address: 1625 West Washington
           Springfield, IL 62701
Name of Writing Lab/Center: Griffin Writing Center
Contact Person: Alan Brown
Computers: Apple
Staff: Teacher, Student Tutors

State: Illinois
Name of School: Hinsdale Central High School
Address: 55th & Grant Streets
           Hinsdale, IL 60521
Name of Writing Lab/Center: Writing Center
Contact Person: Doris Slone
Computers: None
Staff: English Teachers, Student Tutors

State: Illinois
Name of School: Homewood-Flossmoor High School
Address: 999 Kedzie Avenue
           Flossmoor, IL 60422
Name of Writing Lab/Center: English Resource Center
Contact Person: Leslie R. Wilson
Computers: 1 Apple IIe
Staff: 6 Teachers, 24 Student Tutors

State: Illinois
Name of School: Rolling Meadows High School
Address: 2901 Central Road
           Rolling Meadows, IL 60008
Name of Writing Lab/Center: Writing Lab
Contact Person: Tom Schuler

Computers: Apple IIe
Staff: 1 Teacher, 1 Noncertified Staff

State: Illinois
Name of School: Warren Township High School
Address: 300 S. Waukegan Road
       Lake Forest, IL 60045
Name of Writing Lab/Center: The Writing Place
Contact Person: Kim S. Zupec
Computers: IBM PC
Staff: 4 English Teachers

State: Illinois
Name of School: York High School
Address: Elmhurst, IL 60126
Name of Writing Lab/Center: The Write Place
Contact Person: Gloria Nardini

State: Indiana
Name of School: Central High School
Address: 5400 First Avenue
       Evansville, IN 47710
Name of Writing Lab/Center: The Writing Lab
Contact Person: Sharon Sorenson
Computers: None — Cassettes
Staff: 1 Full-time English Teacher

State: Indiana
Name of School: Jefferson High School
Address: 1801 S. 18th Street
       Lafayette, IN 47905
Contact Person: Bonita Fusiek

State: Iowa
Name of School: Burlington Community High School
Address: 421 Terrace Drive
       Burlington, IA 52601
Name of Writing Lab/Center: Communication Resource Center
Contact Person: James Upton
Computers: Apples
Staff: 4 Teachers, Student Volunteers

State: Iowa
Name of School: Hempstead Senior High School
Address: 3715 Pennsylvania
       Dubuque, IA 52001
Contact Person: Steve Fields

State: Kansas
Name of School: Derby Senior High School
Address: 801 E. Madison
          Derby, KS 67037
Name of Writing Lab/Center: The Write Place
Contact Person: Clodell Thomas
Computers: None
Staff: Director and Part-time Tutor

State: Kansas
Name of School: Shawnee Mission North High School
Address: 7401 Johnson Road
          Shawnee Mission, KS 66202
Name of Writing Lab/Center: The Writing Lab
Contact Person: Carol Hailey

State: Maryland
Name of School: Howard High School
Address: 8700 Old Annapolis Blvd.
          Ellicott City, MD 21403
Name of Writing Lab/Center: The Write Place
Contact Person: Linda Sorey, Niki Fortunato
Computers: 10 AT&Ts
Staff: 14 Peers, 25 Staff, 6 Community

State: Massachusetts
Name of School: Belmont High School
Address: 221 Concord Avenue
          Belmont, MA 02178
Name of Writing Lab/Center: Computer-Based Writing
Contact Person: Marilyn Martin
Computers: 16 Apple IIe's
Staff: English Staff

State: Massachusetts
Name of School: Foxborough High School
Address: Foxborough, MA 02035
Name of Writing Lab/Center: Computer Writing Lab
Contact Person: Damian H. Curtiss
Computers: Apple IIe, Raytheon
Staff: Director, Professional Tutors, 20 Students

State: Missouri
Name of School: Hazelwood West Jr./Sr. High School
Address: 6249 Howdershell Road
          Hazelwood, MO 63042
Name of Writing Lab/Center: Hazelwood West Writing Lab
Contact Person: Anne Wright

Computers: 23 Apple IIe's
Staff: English Teachers and Assistant

State: Missouri
Name of School: Kirkwood High School
Address: 801 W. Essex Road
       Kirkwood, MO 63122
Name of Writing Lab/Center: The Writing Center
Contact Person: Penny Stein
Computers: None
Staff: English Teachers, Peer Tutors

State: Missouri
Name of School: Nerinx Hall High School
Address: Webster Groves, MO 63119
Contact Person: Mary Schenkenberg

State: Missouri
Name of School: Parkway North High School
Address: 12860 Fee Fee Road
       Creve Coeur, MO 63146
Contact Person: Rosemary Stocky

State: Missouri
Name of School: Pattonville Senior High School
Address: 2497 Creve Coeur Mill Road
       Maryland Heights, MO 63043
Name of Writing Lab/Center: Writing Center
Contact Person: Barbara Brooks
Computers: 15 Apples
Staff: 2 Directors, 2 Teachers

State: Missouri
Name of School: Vicksburg High School
Address: 501 E. Highway
       Vicksburg, MO 49097
Name of Writing Lab/Center: Language Arts Resource Center
Contact Person: Patricia M. Piua
Computers: None
Staff: English Department

State: Montana
Name of School: Frenchtown High School
Address: Box 117
       Frenchtown, MT 59834
Contact Person: Rick Unruh

State: Nebraska
Name of School: Valentine Middle School
Address: 3rd & Wood Streets
    Valentine, NE 69201
Name of Writing Lab/Center: Valentine Middle School Writing Room
Contact Person: John Neil Graham
Computers: 3 Apples
Staff: 1 Teacher

State: New Jersey
Name of School: Columbia High School
Address: 17 Parker Avenue
    Maplewood, NJ 07040
Name of Writing Lab/Center: Columbia High School Writing Center
Contact Person: Don Lasko
Computers: None
Staff: English Staff Volunteers

State: New Jersey
Name of School: Highland Park High School
Address: N. 5th Avenue
    Highland Park, NJ 08904
Name of Writing Lab/Center: Writing Center
Contact Person: Carol Lefelt
Computers: None
Staff: Teacher and Student Tutors

State: New Jersey
Name of School: Lafayette Middle School
Address: 272 Tanglewood Trail
    Gillette, NJ 07933
Name of Writing Lab/Center: To be Established
Contact Person: M. Wilton
Computers: None
Staff: 1 Teacher

State: New Jersey
Name of School: Millburn Senior High School
Address: 462 Millburn Avenue
    Millburn, NJ 07041
Name of Writing Lab/Center: The Writing Center
Contact Person: Miriam Hoffman
Computers: IBM, Atari
Staff: Teachers, Student Volunteers

State: New Jersey
Name of School: Moorestown High School
Address: Bridgeboro & Stanwick Roads
    Moorestown, NJ 08057

Name of Writing Lab/Center: Writing Center
Contact Person: Tom Goldschmidt
Computers: 2 Apples, 24 IBMs
Staff: 1 Full-time Staff, 35 Peer Tutors

State: New Jersey
Name of School: Oak Knoll School of the Holy Child Jesus
Address: 44 Blackburn Road
          Summit, NJ 07901
Name of Writing Lab/Center: The Writing Center
Contact Person: Harriet Marcus
Computers: Apple IIe
Staff: 1 Part-time Director, 35 Students

State: New Jersey
Name of School: Red Bank Regional High School
Address: 101 Ridge Road
          Little Silver, NJ 07739
Name of Writing Lab/Center: The Writing Center
Contact Person: Pamela B. Farrell
Computers: Apples, IBM, Osborne
Staff: Teacher/Director, Student Volunteers

State: New Jersey
Name of School: Rumson-Fair Haven Regional High School
Address: Ridge Road
          Rumson, NJ 07760
Name of Writing Lab/Center: Writing Lab
Contact Person: William A. Speiser
Computers: Zenith
Staff: English Instructors

State: New Jersey
Name of School: Sterling High School
Address: Warwick Road
          Somerdale, NJ 08083
Name of Writing Lab/Center: Computer Writing Center
Contact Person: Joe Filinuk
Computers: 15 Apple IIe's
Staff: Faculty Volunteers

State: New Jersey
Name of School: Stuart Country Day School
Address: Stuart Road
          Princeton, NJ 08540
Name of Writing Lab/Center: Writing Workshop
Contact Person: Mary Elizabeth Gray
Computers: 15 Apple IIe's
Staff: Teacher

State: New Jersey
Name of School: Vernon Township High School
Address: Glenwood Road
          Vernon, NJ 07462
Name of Writing Lab/Center: Vernon High School Writing Center
Contact Person: George McNally
Computers: 9 IBM PCs
Staff: 3 Teachers, Junior and Senior Tutors

State: New York
Name of School: Huntington High School
Address: Oakwood Road
          Huntington, NY 11743
Name of Writing Lab/Center: Writing Center
Contact Person: Robert Leonard
Computers: Apple IIe
Staff: Teacher, Peer Tutors

State: New York
Name of School: John Marshall High School
Address: 180 Ridgeway Avenue
          Rochester, NY 14615
Name of Writing Lab/Center: Writing Lab
Contact Person: Linda K. Floyd
Computers: 15 TRS-80s
Staff: 1 Teacher

State: New York
Name of School: Mount Markham Senior High School
Address: West Winfield, NY 13491
Name of Writing Lab/Center: Writing Lab
Contact Person: Richard Searles
Computers: Commodore 64
Staff: 2 English Teachers

State: New York
Name of School: Scarsdale High School
Address: Post Road
          Scarsdale, NY 10583
Name of Writing Lab/Center: Writing Center
Contact Person: Amy Levin
Computers: Apple
Staff: Teacher and Student Tutors

State: North Carolina
Name of School: Charlotte County Day Schools
Address: Cannon Campus
          Charlotte, NC 28226

Name of Writing Lab/Center: Writing Center
Contact Person: Jane B. Smith
Computers: Apple IIe
Staff: Faculty and Students

State: North Carolina
Name of School: The Summit School
Address: Reynolds Estates
        Winston-Salem, NC 27106
Name of Writing Lab/Center: The Writing Lab
Contact Person: Dell James
Computers: IBM, Apple
Staff: Writing Coordinator

State: Ohio
Name of School: Austintown Fitch High School
Address: Falcon Drive
        Youngstown, OH 44515
Name of Writing Lab/Center: Writing Lab
Contact Person: Barbara Dios
Computers: 1 Apple
Staff: 5 English Staff, 1 Lab Assistant

State: Ohio
Name of School: Fairmont High School
Address: Kettering, OH 45429
Contact Person: Frank Monturo

State: Ohio
Name of School: Findlay High School
Address: 1200 Broad Avenue
        Findlay, OH 45840
Name of Writing Lab/Center: Writing Lab — The Writing Place
Contact Person: Sherron Davidson
Computers: 17 Apples
Staff: Full-time Teacher, Lab Assistants

State: Ohio
Name of School: Indian Hill High School
Address: 6845 Drake Road
        Cincinnati, OH 45243
Name of Writing Lab/Center: Indian Hill High School Writing Center
Contact Person: Elizabeth Ackley
Computers: None
Staff: Teacher and Trained Student Tutors

State: Ohio
Name of School: Kenmore High School

Address: 2140 13th Street
         Akron, OH 44314
Name of Writing Lab/Center: Kenmore Writing Lab
Contact Person: Rosa Bhakuni
Computers: None
Staff: Teachers, Instructional Assistants

State: Ohio
Name of School: Madeira High School
Address: 7465 Loannes Drive
         Cincinnati, OH 45243
Name of Writing Lab/Center: Writing Assistance Center
Contact Person: D. J. Hammond
Computers: None
Staff: English Teachers (All Day)

State: Oregon
Name of School: West Linn High School
Address: West "A" Street
         West Linn, OR 97068
Name of Writing Lab/Center: Macintosh and Apple Labs
Contact Person: Rose Wallace
Computers: Macintosh, Apples
Staff: Secretary, Teachers

State: Pennsylvania
Name of School: Akiba Hebrew Academy
Address: 223 N. Highland Avenue
         Merion, PA 19066
Name of Writing Lab/Center: Writing Center
Contact Person: Shelley Baum
Computers: None
Staff: 1 Teacher

State: Pennsylvania
Name of School: Elizabethtown Area High School
Address: 600 E. High Street
         Elizabethtown, PA 17022
Name of Writing Lab/Center: Writing and Skill Center
Contact Person: Joan L. Deimler
Computers: 3 Apple IIe's
Staff: 8 Writing-Across-the-Curriculum Staff

State: Pennsylvania
Name of School: J. P. McCaskey High School
Address: 445 North Reservoir Street
         Lancaster, PA 17602
Name of Writing Lab/Center: The Writing Center

Contact Person: Betty Beck
Computers: 10 Apples
Staff: Director, Faculty, Students

State: Pennsylvania
Name of School: Mt. Lebanon Junior High School
Address: 155 Cochran Road
   Pittsburgh, PA 15228
Name of Writing Lab/Center: Writing Lab
Contact Person: Marguerite Kessler
Computers: 3 Franklin Aces
Staff: 1 Writing Clinician

State: Pennsylvania
Name of School: Mt. Lebanon Senior High School
Address: 155 Cochran Road
   Pittsburgh, PA 15228
Name of Writing Lab/Center: The Write Place
Contact Person: Betty Barbara Sipe
Computers: 4 Apple IIe's
Staff: Writing Clinician

State: Pennsylvania
Name of School: Shady Side Academy
Address: 432 Fox Chapel Road
   Pittsburgh, PA 15238
Name of Writing Lab/Center: Writing Centaur
Contact Person: Sarah Eldridge
Computers: IBM
Staff: Director, Student Director, Student Tutors

State: Utah
Name of School: Logan High School
Address: 162 West 100 South
   Logan, UT 84321
Name of Writing Lab/Center: The Writing Room
Contact Person: Pat Stoddart
Computers: IBM PC, IBM XT
Staff: 1 Supervisor, Student Aides

State: Utah
Name of School: Park City High School
Address: 1750 East Highway 248, P. O. Box 1120
   Park City, UT 84060
Name of Writing Lab/Center: The Writing Center
Contact Person: David Partenheimer
Computers: IBM XT
Staff: English Staff, Student Tutors

State: Virginia
Name of School: Salem High School
Address: 400 Spartan Drive
          Salem, VA 24153
Name of Writing Lab/Center: The Writing Center
Contact Person: Jane Brill
Computers: Kaypro II
Staff: Director, Teachers, Students

State: Wisconsin
Name of School: West High School
Address: 30 Ash Street
          Madison, WI 53705
Name of Writing Lab/Center: West High School Writing Lab
Contact Person: Marian Kanable
Computers: None
Staff: Teachers

Editor

Pamela B. Farrell directs the writing center and teaches English and creative writing at Red Bank Regional High School in Little Silver, New Jersey. A Woodrow Wilson National Foundation Fellow, she serves as treasurer of the NCTE Assembly on Computers in English, membership cochair of New Jersey Council of Teachers of English, member of the Editorial Board of *Computers and Composition,* executive board member of the National Writing Center Association, and member of the NCTE Committee to Evaluate Curriculum Guides. She has published numerous articles in professional journals and poems in several anthologies and presented papers and given workshops internationally on writing centers, computers and writing, and writing across the curriculum.

Contributors

Elizabeth Ackley directs the writing center at Indian Hill High School in Cincinnati, Ohio. A Fullbright Scholar and Ohio Writing Project Fellow, she has been both author and consultant for the Macmillan Literature Series. She is also a member of the Executive Board of the National Writing Center Association.

Richard Allen teaches Industrial Arts at Red Bank Regional High School in Little Silver, New Jersey. He is a recipient of the Teacher of the Year Award.

Rosa I. Bhakuni directs the writing lab at Kenmore High School in Akron, Ohio, and also teaches English at the University of Akron.

Lil Brannon is an associate professor of English at the State University of New York at Albany. She serves on the executive committee of the Conference on College Composition and Communication, the delegate assembly of the Modern Language Association, and the consultant/evaluators of the Council of Writing Program Administrators. Her publications include *Writers Writing, Rhetorical Traditions and the Teaching of Writing;* numerous articles in professional journals; and essays in *Current Theory and Research in Composition, Writing Centers: Theory and Administration, Tutoring Writing, Rhetoric and Composition: A Sourcebook for Teachers,* and *Sentence Combining and the Teaching of Writing.*

Ellen H. Brinkley is instructor of English at Western Michigan University. She formerly taught at Madeira High School in Cincinnati, Ohio, where she and two colleagues established a writing center that won NCTE's Center of Excellence award. She has presented papers, given inservice workshops, and authored articles on secondary school writing centers.

Barbara Brooks teaches English and directs the nationally acclaimed writing center at Pattonville High School in Maryland Heights, Missouri. She is currently involved in administrating a state incentive grant for "Peer Writing Tutors Across the Curriculum."

John Neil Graham teaches English and directs the writing lab at Valentine Middle School in Valentine, Nebraska. He works with the Nebraska Writing Project.

Carol Lefelt teaches English and directs the writing center at Highland Park High School in Highland Park, New Jersey. She has published numerous articles, including several in *Writing Lab Newsletter* and continues to give presentations and workshops on the state and national level on writing and writing centers.

Amy K. Levin teaches English and directs the writing center at Scarsdale High School in Scarsdale, New York. She is currently completing a doctoral degree in English literature at the City University of New York. She has presented several workshops locally and nationally.

Henry A. Luce directed the writing center at Monmouth College in West Long Branch, New Jersey. He has published articles in magazines and professional journals, including *Writing Lab Newsletter*. He now works as a technical writer for a pharmaceutical firm and continues to revise his fictional prose for publication.

Harriet Marcus is chairperson of the English Department at Oak Knoll School of the Holy Child Jesus in Summit, New Jersey, where she directs the writing center. Her publications include "The Writing Center: Peer Tutoring in a Supportive Setting" (*English Journal*, September 1984). She is presently enrolled in a Master of Letters program at Drew University.

Betty Barbara Sipe is a writing clinician in the Mt. Lebanon School District in Pittsburgh, Pennsylvania. She has contributed articles to *Classroom Practices in Teaching English* and *Reading Improvement*. A Pennsylvania Writing Project Fellow, she holds a Supervisory Certificate in Communications from Duquesne University.

Sharon Sorenson served as chair of the English Department at Central High School in Evansville, Indiana. She developed the first high school writing lab in the state and has conducted workshops throughout the state to implement the concept in other school systems. Her books are used in writing labs, both in high school and in post-high school.

William A. Speiser has taught all levels of high school English at Rumson-Fair Haven Regional High School in Rumson, New Jersey. Membership cochair of the New Jersey Council of Teachers of English, he has presented papers nationally and published articles in several professional journals. He is particularly interested in helping student writers develop confidence and competence.

Pat Stoddart teaches English and directs the writing center at Logan High School in Logan, Utah. She has collaborated with Joyce Kinkead at the Utah State University writing lab. A frequent presenter at national conferences, she has written several articles for publication in such professional journals as *Writing Lab Newsletter.*

James Upton directs the writing center at Burlington Community High School in Burlington, Iowa. Actively involved in the Southeast Iowa Writing Project and Iowa Writing Project, he has published articles in both *Writing*

Lab Newsletter and *English Journal.* His current interests are writing centers, student tutors, writing in the disciplines, and improved writing instruction in language arts classes. He shares these interests at the many presentations he gives on the state and national level, and he is also a newly elected member of The National Writing Center Executive Board.

Anne Wright, English teacher and codirector of the Gateway Writing Project, helped develop the writing lab, an NCTE Center of Excellence, at Hazelwood West High School in Hazelwood, Missouri. She has written several articles and made presentations at local, state, and national conferences on the use of computers in teaching writing and on setting up writing labs.